SOUTH PASS
And Its Tales

JAMES L. SHERLOCK

WOLVERINE

**GALLERY
BOX 572
GREYBULL, WY 82426
(307) 765-2603**

SECOND EDITION

Published by Wolverine Gallery
First Published by Vantage Press, Inc.
ISBN 0-941875-04-0   (Previously ISBN 533-03296-2)

Printed by Basin Republican Rustler Printing
Basin, Wyoming U.S.A.

SOUTH PASS AND ITS TALES

by James L. Sherlock

Here is a rare find for history buffs: a true account of the birth of a western town in the 1860s and its difficult development from a few shacks into a thriving mining and ranching community. James Sherlock writes from his own childhood memories and from the firsthand stories of friends and relatives; and the spare, rather harrowing tales of South Pass are more fascinating than any novel could be.

Mr. Sherlock writes of attacks by the Sioux as they really were—not the epic spectacles carefully orchestrated by Hollywood stuntmen, but infrequent, violent attacks on isolated small groups, sometimes children, in which the cavalry did not come to the rescue.

Anyone who wants to know what pioneer life was really like will find in this book a treasure trove of knowledge that may soon be lost forever. Mr. Sherlock is one of a handful of experts on the construction of handmade log houses (often fitted together without nails) and of the earliest techniques of gold mining. His parents remember the killing blizzard of 1883, and how Wyoming came to be the first state with woman suffrage. All in all, an engrossing and invaluable piece of Americana. *Thirty-seven photographs.*

This book is dedicated to my grandmother, Janet Smith, my father, John Sherlock, and my uncle, Peter R. Sherlock.

INTRODUCTION

Visitors in South Pass, especially in the twenties, thirties and forties, used to greatly enjoy visiting with Peter Sherlock and were intrigued with his accounts of happenings in earlier days. Mr. Sherlock was often advised to write about them, but there was not much source material, and procrastination is so easy. It was not always because he was unoccupied, because he lived a full life, although blind all during his manhood. It was not that he could not write, because his mother—who with my aunt often spent winters in the later years in warmer climates—went to California one winter and sent Peter a typewriter. With father's assistance, Peter memorized the keyboard and in two weeks wrote a letter of thanks to his mother.

Many of the business letters in connection with the store and livestock business were written by Peter. If it was necessary for father to be out of the store for a short while, Peter knew where much of the canned goods and merchandise on the shelves was kept, and would in such circumstances wait on customers with little help from them. This was before the self-service days, and the merchant would select the goods and place them on the counter for the customer. A loss of one of the senses quite often seems to sharpen the remaining ones, and Peter could usually tell by the sense of touch the difference between a five- and ten-dollar bill.

Cordwood was hauled in four-foot lengths and piled, and Peter would saw it into stove lengths for fuel for the store and the hotel. If father was busy waiting on customers, and someone came in inquiring how to find his way to some place in the country, they would be referred to Peter. Sometimes they would be skeptical as to his ability, but after a few minutes of his directions, which described all roads turning off, details of any landmarks, or gulches and streams to cross, their doubts were soon removed. Living in the country and being very much involved in all the activities of the country and community for twenty years before his accident, Peter had gained an intimate knowledge that was indelibly imbedded in his memory.

Peter had spent one winter attending Creighton College in Nebraska, intending to fit himself for the legal profession, and was an honor student. During his summer vacation, he was working to get money to finance his further education and was employed by a French company, headed by a man named Granier. The project was to build a ditch from Christina Lake to convey water to Rock Creek, supplementing the Rock Creek flow, and then ditching farther downstream from Rock Creek to Atlantic City to get the necessary flow and fall to operate hydraulic operations that would wash the bottom land in Rock Creek through a sluice box and recover the gold in the gravel. While working on this ditch on Slate Creek, in the vicinity of the present U.S. Steel iron mine operations, Peter was working on some rock work in the ditch construction. He placed a shot of dynamite which misfired, and was removing the cap when he touched it off. The blast blew one eye out on his cheek and damaged the other. He was taken to Salt Lake, Omaha and Chicago, but no medical or surgical aid could restore his sight, and after about two years of being able to distinguish daylight from dark, he lost all his vision.

It had been Peter's intention to finish working out the week, about two days more, before returning to college. This turn of events left Peter very despondent, and a careful vigil had to be maintained to prevent suicide. Sawing wood and other activities helped to overcome some of this despondency, and later when a homestead was filed on by Peter, he cut the logs to post length and bored the holes to make the bucks for the buck fence to fence the property. My father and Will Sherlock also worked on this project on Sweetwater River, which was the forerunner of what would afterwards become the South Pass Land & Livestock Company.

A few years ago, in Peoria Heights, Illinois, while visiting my wife's younger sister I saw a picture of the main street section of South Pass, showing the hotel and store, with the caption, "Home of Calamity Jane." South Pass was not the home of Calamity Jane, although she was in this section as were many other colorful characters of the early days. Butch Cassidy danced with my mother in the dance hall built by Will Sherlock and George Flick. Calamity Jane was a niece of Major Gallagher, who lived in the Miners Delight section, and she made her home there for a time.

Mrs. Gallagher taught school in South Pass one or two winters, but Jane was not with them at that time. Calamity Jane was a sister to Mrs. Borner, who came with her husband from the mines and relocated in what is sometimes called Borners Garden, south of the present town of Lander in the Sinks Canyon. Jane was not accepted very cordially by Borner, and consequently her visits were very infrequent and of short duration. These inaccuracies should not be tolerated in the textbooks of the younger generation. Calamity Jane was very warmhearted and kind, in spite of her rough and unladylike actions, and a real workhorse whenever help was needed. During an epidemic in Miners Delight, she was the person who did not contract the ailment, and did most of the work and nursing when all the other women in the camp were sick. Somehow Jane always seemed to be where something special was going on and her help was needed, and this is what earned for her the sobriquet of Calamity Jane. It was Peter's firsthand knowledge from contact with these people or someone whom they knew that was passed on, and for that reason I am moved to attempt to record this story, that the actual facts may be known.

Grandmother (Janet McOmie) came from near Edinburgh, Scotland, with an older brother and his family, and associated with a company of Mormons migrating westward to Utah. She was almost fifteen years of age and walked most of the way from the point of departure at Navoo, Illinois, to Salt Lake City, Utah. There were some hand carts in the company, but for the most part the travelers in this train had horse- or ox-drawn wagons. Grandmother's older brother had a young child, and grandmother carried the child in her arms much of the way across the trail. This child, Nettie later became the wife of J.J. (Bob) Marrin in later years. In Utah she met Richard Sherlock, whom she later married. Sherlock had come from London, England. He had brought his family—consisting of a wife, a two-year-old daughter, and Peter, a babe in arms—to the South Pass Country in the spring of 1868.

A ferry across Sweetwater was in operation, and Sherlock bought it, but in a few weeks the mountain snow run-off was over and the stream was easily fordable. Realizing the folly of the purchase and the error of the investment, he moved his family to South Pass, where he worked at numerous projects. While working in the spring of the year at a sawmill on Willow Creek about three miles above South Pass City he caught a bad cold which turned into pneumonia, from which he died.

Mrs. William (Boss) Tweed was the first white woman to live in the town of South Pass, and Mrs. Kime and Mrs. Chittim may have been here when grandmother arrived. Grandmother leased a building that had been operated for a short time as a hotel but had been closed down. She reopened the hotel and later married a second time. James Smith was also an Englishman, having emigrated from Ireland. He was quite a prominent figure in the community and a very eccentric individual. He wore buckskin underwear the year around, made from tanned antelope or deer hide, the antelope being lighter and easier to wash, and so preferred. When Smith got a new pair of boots, he would stand in Willow Creek about half a day, then wear them on his feet until dry so that they would conform to his feet and be comfortable until worn out.

Smith showed considerable favoritism to his children and was mean to the stepchildren. Therefore the boys, Peter, Will and John, left home and fended for themselves at an early age. Smith made two trips to London, endeavoring to sell stock in mining ventures, but was not very successful. Upon his death, the boys again returned home and became associated with their mother in the family business operations.

As a child, grandmother would sometimes tell me about the town's businesses, naming them in order along the street, but in my youthfulness, they did not seem of much importance to me. I gained considerable knowledge of South Pass from her, but more from my uncle Will, my father, and most of all from my blind uncle, Peter. From these sources I have tried to write an authentic story of happenings in South Pass, as some could probably be obtained from no other source today.

My mother's side of the family arrived in the South Pass country about ten years after my father's family. Grandfather Carr was of predominantly Pennsylvania Dutch descent, a man of medium size, a natural-born farmer, and a Civil War veteran; he was seen for many years at the head of the parade in the Lander Pioneer Days celebration, driving his team of mules hitched to a cannon. His military service was mainly in actions against the warring tribes of Indians who were taking advantage of the Civil War to further their campaigns against the white man's intrusion into the west.

Grandmother Carr, mostly of Irish descent, was a small woman, a very active person, a hard worker, and the mother of eight children. Her maiden name was Rhoades. The family came from Colorado to Wyoming in a covered wagon. Mother and a brother rode horseback and drove the stock. The Carr family lived around the Lewiston country during some of the summers, where the cows were brought to forage and butter was made. Milk and butter were sold to the miners in the country. This is where father met mother. Mother was a small woman, very much like grandmother, weighing around a hundred pounds. Mother enjoyed recounting stories of the early days in the country.

From this introduction, you will be aware of my deep interest in the country about which I write.

ACKNOWLEDGMENTS

The author wishes to acknowledge the assistance of Gary Stephenson, Tom Shaffer, the Wyoming Recreation Commission, and Lula Topham in securing some of the pictures from their files for this manuscript; also the constant and untiring urging of my wife to complete this story.

SOUTH PASS AND ITS TALES

CHAPTER

I

Some persons thoroughly enjoy nomadic living, but those of us who do not, usually form a great attachment for the place of our birth and childhood. This fascination with the enchantment and charm of bygone days carries me back in nostalgic reminiscence. I am moved to invite you to accompany me along the streets and places in the adjoining neighborhood, that I might share with you some of my knowledge of the happenings and events of the locality.

When I was at the store, our customers found the few remaining buildings of considerable interest. While I was Worshipful Master of Wyoming Lodge No. 2 at Lander, we had a picnic in the summer of 1956 for members, families and friends. We made a brief tour of the town. Later, I was invited to take the Fremont County Homemakers around the town, and on another occasion, the Sweetwater County Historical Society accompanied me. In 1970 the Lodge held a dedication ceremony for the reconstruction project of the old home of Wyoming Lodge No. 2, with the joint participation of the Lincoln County Historical Society. At that time, too, we toured the town. On each of these occasions, some members have suggested and even urged me to write of the incidents that I related to them, and so I believe they may be of interest to you.

The search for gold was the lodestone that caused the creation of this settlement. The mineralized character of this country adjacent to the overland trail was observed by these immigrants.

A soldier of fortune came to this section from Georgia in the 1840s or 1850s; 1842 seems to be the generally accepted date of his first journey. Not finding the dreamed-of riches, he returned to Georgia when the wintery weather approached, but his success, although meager, led him to return again. On the next trip, he met with more success but again returned to Georgia for the winter. On his third return, the trail ends. There is no record of his demise, but his failure to return to Georgia would indicate that he may have suffered and succumbed to sickness, encountered a savage tomahawk, or perished in the inclement weather.

There are several rumors and accounts of prospecting parties in the 1860s but the real discovery that led to settlement— as related by those who made it, and friends and associates of these persons—came about in this manner:

A small detachment of soldiers was dispatched from Ft. Bridger, to pursue and capture some horse thieves who had raided a Mormon settlement in Utah and stolen their horses. The horse thieves were heading north, presumably for their hideout in the Hole-in-the-Wall country in northern Wyoming. The detachment followed their trail into the Lander Valley without overtaking them; and because there were abundant signs that many Indians were in the valley and the detachment was few in number, the men decided that prudence was the better part of valor, so the chase was abandoned.

On their return trip, camp for the night was set up on Willow Creek below the present site of South Pass City. Many of the recruits in the service were prospectors, mountain men, trappers and guides. Some of the party panned the gravel in the stream at the campsite. A few colors were found in their pan, and some of the men declared that they would serve out their enlistment and return in the fall to make a more extensive investigation.

Tom Ryan was a member of this party, but his term of enlistment did not end until the spring of 1867. It was agreed that he would serve out his enlistment, after which he would join the party; however he was to be included in the party. (Tom was an individual inclined to prevaricate, as is evidenced in a story told by him: The first time he came to South Pass, he came to the hill on the south side of Willow Creek, and it was so full of snow that he rode his mule through the soft snow that filled the gully from hill to hill and he did not know he had gone through the depression until he reached the top of the Carissa hill and looked back and saw the tracks where he had gone into the snow. The valley was level full and he had not even disturbed the snow on the top.)

The party was outfitted at Ft. Bridger and set up camp late in the fall of 1866 after the Indians had gone into winter camp. In a short while the source of the gold was determined to be what was afterwards named the Carissa Gulch, which came into Willow Creek at the campsite.

The quartz outcropping was soon located and, via crude hand mortars, the rock was crushed and panned, and several thousand dollars' worth was extracted from the rich ore by this method during the winter of 1866-67.

With spring came the new grass, and since this provided feed for the horses, the miners realized it would soon be time for the Indians to make their appearance in these hills. The miners had their horses hobbled or picketed, but one of the party, Captain Lawrence, left his horse foot-free, as he knew it would not leave the other horses. It was his custom to go out in the morning and bring the horses to camp. One morning a shot was heard, and upon investigation, Lawrence was found shot to death. Securing their horses, the miners quickly broke camp and fled. They were forced to engage in a running fight with the Indians, who pursued them to the Burnt Ranch on Sweetwater, where another of the party, a man named Tony Shields, was killed. The Indians gave up the fight here, and the party was able to reach Ft. Bridger without further trouble.

After their arrival at Ft. Bridger, the news of the discovery spread rapidly, and a party of sufficient size to assure protection from the Indians was soon on its way to the mines. From this beginning, the population soon increased, and a rather orderly town was developed, with a summertime population of between four and five thousand people located in the immediate vicinity. About the same number also occupied the towns of Atlantic City, Hamilton (later known as Miners Delight), and Lewiston, making a total of between ten and twelve thousand people in the area in 1870 and 1871.

This population fluctuated with the season, with probably ten to twenty percent remaining the year round in the early years.

Houses were erected to provide shelter from the wintery blasts, and some order was followed in establishing roads and streets. The main street followed the general course of the small stream known as Willow Creek and was designated South Pass Avenue.

In the townsite as established by the Federal Gold Mining Company in 1902, this street was designated Main Street. The company's s map also shows Smith Street, South Pass Street, B Street, S Street, and Carissa Street. The intention seems to have been to use the original street names, but it is clear that the names and locations of the streets were not associated accurately with the original locations. The original locations extended beyond the boundaries of this 1902 establishment. The early locations included A, B, C, Smith, Dakota, and Custer avenues; Washington, Jefferson, Colfax, Price, and Grant streets; a street named after another president—which one I am unable to state for certain—and perhaps some more streets.

We will start our journey at the upper end of South Pass Avenue, where we find the ditch that carried the water to an arrastre (sometimes referred to by the miners as a Rastus). The arrastre is almost obliterated. This was a structure of Spanish origin used to crush ore in the recovery of metals from the rock. It consisted of a stone or brick tub. I believe the sides of this one were made of brick, the only arrastre I know of that utilized this material in its construction. Most of the tubs

South Pass City, 1870. Jackson photo.

South Pass City about 1900.

South Pass City, 1927.

were made of granite rocks, but there was a brick kiln about half a mile up Willow Creek on the south side of the creek. Brick clay was dug and brick was burned at this location.

A hole for a bearing was made in the center rock of the tub, in which a vertical wooden shaft was placed. On this vertical timber two and sometimes four arms were horizontally attached above the rim of the tub. Chains suspended by eye bolts from the end of these arms extended into the tub, and on this end of the chains granite stones were attached by means of eye bolts, in which holes had been drilled, and the bolts fastened by pouring hot lead into the hole around the bolt. Above these arms were a series of spokes on some structures and a large wooden wheel on others, which transmitted the power to rotate the vertical shaft. The top of the shaft was fashioned to provide a bearing in the timbered structure, so that when revolved, the stone drags would drag on the bottom of the tub. The usual source of power was furnished by an overshot or undershot waterwheel, but in a few instances, a small steam engine was utilized on some installations in the district. Where water was used, a ditch was dug and a flume built in the overshot wheels to operate the water-wheel, which was mounted by the side of the tub. Power from the horizontal shaft was applied by a series of spokes interlacing with the spokes on the vertical shaft, or from the wooden drive wheel and a belt. Rope was sometimes used as a belt for this type of drive. A small stream of water was fed into the tub, and ore was shoveled in. As the stones dragging in the tub ground the ore, the lighter parts of the ground ore ("tailings") would be carried away in the overflow, while the heavier metals settled to the bottom. To recover the metals, the operator would have a clean-up by diverting the water from the operations and cleaning the bottom of the tub, removing the remaining waste material by means of a gold pan.

A street came down the Mohammet Gulch and crossed South Pass Avenue, continuing up the hill on the south side of town. This was probably A Street.

Careful observation will reveal the location of some of

the houses in this part of town. A dump of considerable size up the gulch on the west side of A Street was created by excavation of a shaft and drifting of tunnels on a claim that was known as the Mohammet. On the east side of the gulch from the Mohammet, is a shaft that was sunk to a depth of about fifty feet, but not much ore was taken from this claim. This claim was called the Charles Dickens.

These claims were sold to the Federal Gold Mining Company, and are probably an extension of the Carissa Vein, as this vein and the Miner's Delight Vein are the most well defined leads in the district. Following the vein across Willow Creek on the hill southwest, is the claim known as the Robert Emmett, afterwards named the Gould and Curry, and later renamed the Franklin. There was a shaft house on the Mohammet and several log structures on the Franklin or Gould & Curry, but most of them are gone now. The logs in the Mohammet were used for fuel for the boilers at the Carissa. One spring, the cordwood supply at the Carissa was exhausted while there was yet too much snow in the mountains to make supplies there accessible.

When Tom Ryan arrived at South Pass after being mustered out of the service, he found that he had not been included in the partnership locations. From the geological formations, he endeavored to follow the Carissa Vein and established his claim, which he called the Carter Lode. This claim produced some of the best high-grade ore in the district. The gold in the quartz had a wire-like quality, and the ore was very pockety—perhaps a pocket of about a cubic foot of very rich ore surrounded by mediocre ore, these pockets being very unpredictable. The high-grade ore was ideal specimen rock.

A ten-stamp steam power mill with a copper-plate amalgam-recovery process was built on Willow Creek a short distance north of the Carter Lode, and much of Ryan's ore was milled here. The mill later became the property of Peter Sherlock and J.J. Marrin, and in later years was sold to the B & H Mining Company, which I now understand has been acquired by the Wyoming Recreation Commission. The B & H Mining

The Franklin Mine.

Mill on Willow Creek above South Pass.

Company moved the mill to Palmetto Gulch and set up one battery of five stamps. That is its location today.

The building, housing the mill on Willow Creek was made of rough lumber, with the cracks in the joining boards battened and the framework made of 10 by 10 timbers square, hewn and mortised by hand. Their exact fit clearly displayed the wonderful craftsmanship of a broad-axe expert who possessed patience, skill, and devotion to the hard labor necessary to produce a building that would meet with his approval and satisfaction.

There are several shafts on the Carter (now Franklin) claim. And it carries another tale that may be of historical interest, although it happened in later years. A man named Edein had a farm on the Wind River Indian Reservation and was called to service in World War I. In the service he struck up acquaintance with a man from Chicago, who became a buddy and expressed a considerable interest in Wyoming. He was a man of some means and became a partner with Edein in his ventures, furnishing investment capital.

It appears that this man, Knapp by name, was led to believe that some of his money was also invested in mining ventures. After a period of several years, Knapp arranged to come to Wyoming to see some of his holdings. Knapp was met on his arrival in Lander by Edein, and they at once set out for the mines.

While they were looking down a shaft, the rotted timbers on the collar of the shaft gave way, and Knapp fell down the shaft, apparently hitting his head on a rock and receiving a fatal blow, according to Edein's story. Edein came down to the Smith-Sherlock Store at South Pass to get help, and my older brother and Billy Bilcox took ropes and went to the shaft to remove the body from the hole. There was no sign of life, and the body was brought to South Pass and authorities notified of the accident. The coroner's jury reported the verdict to be death from a blow on the head by a sharp object. Several months later, a prospector's hand pick was found at Edein's ranch, with blood and hair on the point, and Edein was

KEY TO MAP

1. Arrastre
2. Mahommet Mine
3. Charles Dickens Mine
4. Bayers House
5. Bayers Barn
6. Wygal House
7. Converse House
8. Converse outhouse
9. Hinnman House
10. Basco Cabin
11. Freund Building; Masonic Lodge
12. Restaurant
13. Bayers second barn
14. Schoolhouse (old location)
15. Blacksmith shop
16. Williams House
17. Marrin House
18. Two-story house
19. Pioneer Brewery
20. Tunnel and spring
21. Brigham Barrows House
22. Harsch Blacksmith Shop
23. Matson House
24. First jail
25. Dance hall
26. Wholesale liquor store
27. Dr. Lovejoy House
28. Antone Stubo House
29. Antone's Garden
30. First Schoolhouse
31. Tibbal's Cabin
32. Bathhouse
33. Leckie House
34. Well Curbing
35. Carissa Saloon
36. White Swan
37. Smith-Sherlock Store
38. Kidder Hotel location
39. Cellar
40. Sherlock House
41. Blacksmith shop
42. Courthouse
43. Log House (first white child born here)
44. Bilcox well house
45. Smith House
46. Bilcox chicken coop
47. Large building (probably a store)
48. Brick Moore Cabin
49. Gillespie House
50. Renicker Cabin
si. Dumphrey Cabin
52. Esther Morris Home and Office
53. Wells-Fargo Express Office
54. Illif Bank Building
55. Grecian Bend Saloon
56. Sherlock Hotel
57. Irvin House
58. Pool Hall
59. Baskin & DeWolf office
60. Theatre
61. Blacksmith shop
62. Episcopal Church
63. Beer garden
64. Ticknor Store
65. Millinery Store (Esther Morris)
66. Barn and carriage shed
67. Black Horse Livery Stable
68. Pest House
69. Jail
70. William (Boss) Tweed Home
71. Brewery
72. Charcoal ovens
73. Blacksmith shop
74. Residences on Custer Ave. Hillside.
75. Brown House
76. George Volmer House & Barn
77. New School House
78. Carissa Mine

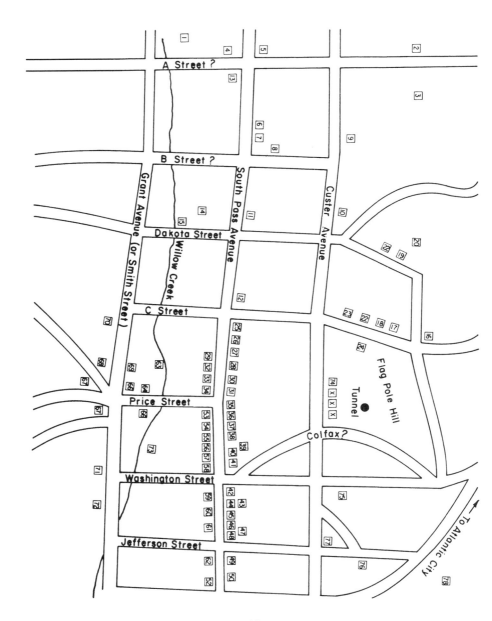

A Street ?

B Street ?

Grant Avenue (or Smith Street)

South Pass Avenue

Custer Avenue

Dakota Street

Willow Creek

C Street

Price Street

Washington Street

Jefferson Street

Colfax?

Flag Pole Hill

Tunnel

To Atlantic City

brought to trial, convicted, and sentenced to a term in the penitentiary.

I have constructed a rough sketch of the town and streets as they may have been to help us on our journey through the town.

The house now standing on the upper end of South Pass Avenue was one of the older houses in the town, but I do not know who occupied it first. My father lived in it one or two winters while he was engaged in hauling ore from the Carissa mine to the mill down the creek, for Bolivar Roberts. In my recollection, it was the home of a mail contractor, a Prussian who held contract for the carrying of mail from Lander to Pinedale. (This was before Sublette County was formed, so there was considerable necessity for passenger and mail service and communications to that end of the county.) This contractor, Albert Bayers, had a number of children; some of their descendants live in Lander, Pinedale, and Rock Springs. Mrs. Bayers was a very capable woman and often drove the mail coach or sleigh; she could be depended on to get the mail through in adverse weather conditions better than Mr. Bayers or some of the other drivers. She also had a forceps to relieve the pain of severe toothache by extraction of the offending tooth. Albert Bayers was quite often a source of considerable amusement to the passengers, and I remember the joy created when a passenger related her experience coming through the Red Canyon. Pointing to an object some distance up on the hill, Bayers inquired "Is dat rock up on de hill a horse or a cow?"

A barn which was back of the house across A Street and north of South Pass Avenue was burned to the ground. It had been used to stable the horses used on the stage line. The fire was well under way before the whinnying of a terrified horse aroused the family. This was one of the finest horses used on the stage line route and was stabled while the other horses were in a corral outside. The horse died in the fire before it was possible to remove him.

It was about this time that the youngest daughter, Celia,

contracted diphtheria and passed away. Dr. Maghee came to South Pass from Lander with antitoxin, and all of the children in the town got the shots. This Dr. Maghee was in charge of the Wyoming State Training School for a while and was able to reduce the frequency of seizures among the patients through medication; he was one of the pioneers in this program.

The Bayers house is now owned by Mrs. Zoie Fuller. The Bayers family came to South Pass from the Pinedale and Big Piney section.

The next house that I remember on the north side of South Pass Avenue was a log house with a roof built with poles and covered with dirt. It was occupied by a family named Wygals, some of whom now live in Filer, Idaho. The next occupant was William Carr. The houses west of this house were abandoned or removed, and as the Carr family increased in size, the house was added on to until it was more than twice its original size. Smaller units were built back of it, some dug into the hillside. When the family left South Pass, there were thirteen children, the fourteenth child born after leaving South Pass; so it took considerable building to keep up with the family's growth.

There was a street on the hill back of the small cabins, which ran parallel to South Pass Avenue; this street may have been Custer Avenue. Custer Avenue was located on the hillside east from Mormon Gulch, but it may have terminated at what was probably C Street, a north and south street located along Mormon Gulch and continuing to the hill on the south side of town.

B Street may have been located on the east side of this Carr house, beginning at Custer Avenue and crossing South Pass Avenue, continuing up the hill on the south.

There was probably another house or two between this Carr, or Wygal, house and the Converse house as South Pass Avenue was built up solid on both sides of the street, the length of the town, but the next house I remember was a log structure, almost square in shape. There was a well in front of the house, close to the street, while the outhouse was behind

15

and east of the house, at the foot of the hill. This house was occupied by Professor Converse, who forsook his profession to seek riches in the goldfields of this community. From stories about this gentleman, I would judge him to be quite a character in the life of the community and town. He stated that the general character of the soil in this section was abundant in potash, due to its volcanic geological formation. A rawboned, rugged individual, it was his custom to arise early, don a robe, and make his way across the street to a beaver dam in Willow Creek for a morning dip. This was his usual procedure the year round, the only variation being that in the winter he had to take an axe to cut a hole in the ice before getting his bath. The healthful benefits can not be denied, for he was past ninety years of age when leaving South Pass City and could read a newspaper with the naked eye. As for eyesight, he contended that the muscles of the eye had a tendency to flatten the ball, and if a person would press and massage the eyes to maintain their orbital shape, optical aids would not be necessary.

Converse made a wood box for our hotel kitchen, and I carried many a load of wood to fill it. Legs held the box about sixteen inches from the floor, and the box measured about twenty-eight by thirty-four inches, with a depth of about four-teen inches. It was placed in the corner of the kitchen close by the stove, and wood was stacked five and a half feet high in the winter, not quite so high during the summer months. Although Professor Converse left South Pass City about the time of my birth, the sturdy construction of this wood box was a marvel to me, as it remained a very serviceable box when I left South Pass City, after at least sixty years of use.

One of the occupants of the Converse house in my time was the Bates family. Mrs. Bates was my aunt. Some of the descendants live in Lander now.

CHAPTER

II

There was a house on the hill north of the street that, as stated before, may have been Custer Avenue. There were a number of houses on this street along the hill, but most of them were gone before my time, and evidence of their location is gradually being obliterated. This house of which I speak was north and a little east of the Converse house. It was a two-room frame house with a shed addition at the back. The Hinnman residence was in this vicinity, and it is my firm belief that this was the house, although I have no definite knowledge. Washington Mallory Hinnman appears to have been a very energetic man, thought to have come from a little town called Broken Bow, in Nebraska. He traveled along the emigrant trails, establishing trading posts, setting up saw mills, and engaging in general business activities from Nebraska to the West Coast and along the coast in California, Washington and Oregon, then drifting back to South Pass City with the activities around this section. Here, he had a sawmill on Slate Creek, a gold mill, perhaps a five-stamp mill located on the Hermit below the town of South Pass City, and with partners incorporated a toll road between South Pass City and Atlantic City, also another up Slate Creek. There were plans to establish a townsite on Slate Creek, but only a few houses were ever built there.

The toll and wagon road incorporation was one of the first, if not the first, corporation in the Wyoming Territory. The Atlantic City and South Pass City Wagon and Toll Road Company was incorporated under and pursuant to a legislative act of Dakota Territory entitled "An act to regulate incorporations", approved January 1, 1869. It was incorporated with capital stock of twenty-five thousand dollars with a par value of $100. per share. Articles of incorporation were filed by Jas. W. Menefee and C.H. Fry in Carter County, Dakota Territory, on May 15, 1869. I do not know when the Slate Creek road was incorporated, but it was after this.

Hinnman was the first Worshipful Master of Wyoming Lodge No. 2 when it was held under dispensation from Nebraska Grand Lodge with the number of 28 U.D. It was in the Hinnman shed of this house, after it was abandoned, that my brothers and friends, with that inborn mining instinct, decided to do some mining. There was an under-floor cellar about four feet square and two and a half feet deep which was likely used to store potatoes and vegetables. By means of a baling wire, we anchored a pulley to a roof rafter, and with a quarter-inch rope and a ten-pound lard pail, operations began. The board lid in the floor covering the cellar, which was about three foot square, was removed, and a miner with a short-handled shovel descended into the mine. The miner—sometimes there were two—loaded the bucket with dirt, and by means of the rope which when pulled would ring a bell in the hoist house, signaled for the bucket to be hoisted to the surface. When it reached the floor level, another hand would grasp the pail and carry the dirt out to the dump. The bucket was then returned for a refill. This excavation continued down about two feet when pay dirt was struck. A cigar box which was made to hold one hundred of the common cigars as made at that time, was hoisted to the surface and the contents examined. It contained specimen quartz rock pieces from one-half to one and a half inches in size, all of which showed considerable free gold. The shaft was deep enough that a ladder would be required for continued operations, and taking the nuggets home provided a clue to our activities. There followed a paternal investigation, whereupon it was determined that there was danger of a cavein if operations were to continue without proper timbering, so we had to abandon the project. Somehow I have always felt that this was the Hinnman residence, as it was on this approximate location; however I have no definite knowledge that this was the house. This house was used in later years by a Scotsman named Colin MacPherson Spiers, who had a homestead on the head of Fish Creek, and would use the house when coming to town to stay overnight or for a day or so.

Another house east of this house was built after some of the other buildings were gone: a one-room cabin built by Joe Basco, who came to South Pass City at a later time. Joe was a man of small stature, perhaps five feet two inches, and muscular but not large. He was of Austrian descent. When excited, he talked very fast in a squeaky, high-pitched voice. He was a very capable blacksmith, and in the earlier days was very busy. Later, when business was slow, he left South Pass City and homesteaded on Oregon Gulch where it runs into Sweetwater at Burnt Ranch. He would come to the shop when notified that his services were needed. He also derived a great deal of pleasure trading horses with any Indians who chanced to be passing through the country, and had quite a few horses that ranged around the Sweetwater. Later, he had a few head of cattle. Joe was on call for the Pacific Springs shop where Halter and Flick had established a stopover, or way house, a general store, saloon and associated enterprises. Although it was a small settlement, gambling, drinking and wild women offered entertainment in abundance.

Back on South Pass Avenue, we now find the replica construction of the Freund building. This building owned by the Freund brothers was partially destroyed by fire, and the portion that could be used was salvaged and used when the blacksmith shop was added on the north side of the old Carissa Mine Shaft House. There was a log with the square and compass carved into it in the wall back of the forge in the shop. This structure was removed when Midwest Mines replaced the mill with the Dexter Mill that was moved from Atlantic City.

The reason for this carved square and compass was because the upper floor of the building was rented by Wyoming Lodge No. 2, and the meetings were held here. The minutes of these early meetings indicate that the Lodge experienced difficulty in paying the rental on this building, and it was often necessary for the Lodge to request rental reductions, which were granted by the Freund brothers, who were members of the order.

The building was constructed of logs on the lower story, with the customary false front and central doorway, and with large windows on either side of the entrance. The upper story was of rough lumber, probably sawed by the Hinnman sawmill, with the joining board joints covered with a board batten. The log with the square-and-compass carving was incorporated as the top-sill timber across the back, to which the upper end of the wall boards were nailed with the square wrought-iron nails that were used at that time. The front room of the lower story was the display and sales room of the Freund brothers, who dealt in guns, pistols, cutlery, sporting goods, fixed and loose ammunition, E.I. DuPont de Nemours sporting and mining powder, and were the sole agents in the entire West for the Winchester Patent Repeating Rifle and Carbine, called the eighteen-shooter, according to their advertisement in the *Sweetwater Mines* of June 19, 1869. The back room was the warehouse and shop where guns were repaired.

The South Pass City establishment was a branch of the Cheyenne office. Browning, who was employed by the Freund Brothers, worked here and began his work on the Browning automatic rifle that was later adopted by the government for the armed forces. When leaving South Pass City, the Freunds moved to Ogden, Utah, and later, the ownership was acquired by Browning through purchase.

Entrance to the upper story of the building was by means of a peculiarly constructed stairway on the east side at the south end of the building. Three steps in the boardwalk brought the person to the level of the porch in front of the

Replica of Lodge Hall — Ancient Free and Accepted Masons #28, U.D. Nebraska; now Wyoming #2, Lander.

building. Five additional steps going north and out from the building the width of the steps, brought a person to a platform from which, against the side of the building, ran a flight of seven steps going south to another landing, from which a door provided entrance to the lodge room. In the reconstruction, this arrangement has not been followed, as the twelve steps are divided into flights of six steps each, instead of the five-and-seven divisions.

Washington Mallory Hinnman was appointed the first Worshipful Master of this lodge, at a communication on December 6, 1869. The Senior Warden office was filled by brother Morris Appel; L. Engle was Junior Warden, C.A. Smith, Treasurer; F. Gillman, Secretary; F. H. Bannoll, Senior Deacon; H.C. Sedgewick, Junior Deacon, and E.G. Brown, Tyler *pro-tem*.

Brothers Shakspear, Gillman, and Bannoll were appoint-

21

ed as a committee to draw up by laws and rules of order. This communication was held after a dispensation from the Grand Lodge of Nebraska, with the lodge to be known as Wyoming Lodge, U.D. ("under dispensation"). On August 2, 1870, the Lodge became Wyoming Lodge No. 28, under the jurisdiction of the Grand Lodge of Nebraska, at which time institution and installation proceedings were conducted by A.E. Cutler, Past Master of Cleveland Lodge No. 2, Chicago, Illinois, who held a dispensation from Most Worshipful Master H.P. Deuel, Grand Master of the Grand Lodge of Nebraska. At their installation, W.M. Hinnman was installed as Worshipful Master; A.K. Morrison, Senior Warden; S.J. Connell, Junior Warden; C.A. Smith, Treasurer; G.F. Gillman, Secretary; G.W. Dixon, Senior Deacon; and J.F. Lightburn, Junior Deacon. My father showed me the location of the original building, and the rock foundation was clearly visible. I placed a small stone at each corner and a crude schist slab marker on the location in 1920. I was not a member of the fraternity then and the marker erroneously marked the site as that of the First Masonic Temple of Wyoming Lodge No. 1, Ancient Free and Accepted Masons.

Captain H.G. Nickerson had placed a marker at the site of the office and home of Esther Morris, and it proved to be of considerable interest to the general public. The marker that I had placed was not adequate or fitting, and I therefore contacted Richard LeRossignol who in 1923 was Senior Warden when I became a member of the order, and one of my better friends. I approached him with the idea that the Lodge might be interested in providing a more appropriate and fitting marker on the site. He at once contacted a member who had previously served the Lodge as Worshipful Master and later as Grand Master of the Grand Lodge of Wyoming, William Dickinson. Brother Dickinson approved the idea, and the matter was brought before the Lodge in their regular meeting at which it was decided that a bronze plaque mounted on a durable base would be the most appropriate. LeRossignol appraised me of the action on the matter, and I suggested mounting the plaque on a granite stone I knew of and that I thought would be suit-able. This stone had been hauled in from a few miles above South Pass City by being suspended between the front- and rear-running gears of a wagon on logs placed on either side of the bolsters. It would probably weigh in the neighborhood of six tons. I moved the stone to its new location by this same method.

It had stood in the center of the town, where it had been used in a Fourth of July drilling contest between South Pass City and the rival town of Atlantic City in 1904 or 1905. The members on the South Pass team were Dan Carmody and Jack Hollihan, and the Atlantic team consisted of Peter Gustafson and Emmet Connell. One man would swing the double jack (a heavy sledgehammer) and the other man would turn the drill. The members of the team would change jobs when the man on the hammer got tired. After drilling a specified time, the depth of the holes were measured, and the deepest hole determined the winning team. As the story goes, Hollihan, who was a large, burly man, developed an attack of acute indigestion dur-ing the excitement and grueling labor in the contest, and his small, plucky Irish partner continued alone, using the hammer like a single jack (a smaller hammer designed for use when drilling alone, wherein the driller turned the drill with one hand and hammered with the other) but the hammer was heavy and cumbersome, and as there was some time remaining in the contest, the two-man team passed him, so that at the end of the designated time, the Atlantic team had the deepest hole. The drill holes are visible on the right-hand face of the stone on the east side. It was necessary to move the stone from the central location when the replica building was erected, and the stone is now embedded in the ground at the northeast corner of the building. The bronze plaque was attached with expansion bolts at the four corners inserted in holes drilled in the stone by Thomas McGrath, William Mathisen, R. LeRossignol and myself. This marker was fittingly dedicated by the Grand Lodge of Wyoming on August 21, 1926.

The desire to have proper authority and jurisdiction over

the site and marker prompted Wyoming Lodge No. 2 to write to John C. Spry, President of the Federal Gold Mining Company, about acquisition of the lot. (It then was included in the plat of South Pass City when the Federal Gold Mining Co. obtained patent to the Wolverine Lode Mining Claim and laid out the townsite.) In reply, Mr. Spry stated that he had great respect and high esteem for the Masonic Order, although he was not a member, that he knew the lot and would forward the deed as a donation. This he did, and the deed is now in the possession of Wyoming Lodge No. 2, at Lander, Wyoming.

The importance of the role played by fraternal organizations in the life of the community might well be illustrated in my grandmother's talk with visitors in later years, when they would ask her if she did not find life in a rowdy, boisterous mining town to be extremely dangerous and difficult. Her reply was that she felt more uneasiness now than she did then. There were the courts of law and law enforcement personnel, and the civic groups and fraternal orders, the Eagles and the Masons, were always ready to assist in promoting justice and lawful order in the camps, and she had always been treated with proper respect.

The subject of construction of the replica of the original building—in view of the statewide interest in preservation of the history of South Pass City—was presented to the members of Wyoming Lodge No. 2. The project was adopted, and today a replica occupies the location of the original building.

After the replica had been constructed, it was discovered that the Federal Gold Mining Company lots, as laid out in the townsite plat, did not coincide with the lots as laid out in the earlier plats, and that the building stood partially on a lot for which the Lodge did not have a deed. The land was claimed by the Pioneer Carrissa Gold Mines, a company of avaricious tendencies in contrast to the old Federal Gold Mining Company, and it was necessary to purchase this additional lot at a cost of one thousand dollars, the lot having a twenty-five-foot frontage on South Pass Avenue. An annual picnic has been held for several years and the profit from the sale of the picnic dinners go to the restoration fund; the restoration committee intends to continue this custom and equip the hall with replicas of the furnishings of the old hall. Some of the original furnishings are in the Masonic Temple in Lander, Wyoming. The original altar was constructed from wood obtained from packing cases in which merchandise was shipped to Cosgriff's store in South Pass, from the railroad shipping point in Point of Rocks. This is authenticated by visible lettering on some of the boards on the inside of this old furnishing. As the railroad construction progressed, Rock Springs was a closer point for shipment of merchandise to the mines.

There are signs of another building foundation east of the Freund Building, but I have no knowledge of what it might have been. Dakota Street must have crossed South Pass Avenue on the east side of this building and continued across Willow Creek to Smith (Grant) Street.

The June 19, 1869, issue of the *Sweetwater Mines* carries publication of town ordinance, Section 12, relating to the grading of South Pass Avenue between Price and Dakota streets, establishing the grade as follows:

Beginning at a point in Price Street, as marked by a stake, and running to Dakota Street. The stakes will be placed so that property owners on the north side of South Pass Avenue will be required to lower their side so as to correspond with the grade established as run by the stakes. The property owners on the south side will be governed accordingly, and that the said property owners are required to have such work completed by the 15th day of July, A.D., 1869, and any property owner failing or refusing to comply with this ordinance, the Board of Trustees will have such work done and hold the property, and sell the same according to law, to pay the expense of grading in front of said property.

This ordinance is signed by John Boyd, President of the Board, and attested by W.F. Edwards, Clerk.

Although there was another or possibly two more buildings between Dakota Street and the building by the small stream crossing South Pass Avenue, I have no knowledge of who may have occupied them. The building by the small spring stream, which was also the corner where C Street intersected South Pass Avenue, was a rather large structure, with the customary large windows on either side of the door. In the front was a dining room with the kitchen at the back, which had a small underfloor storage cellar. The building had a ceiling that I would estimate as nine or ten feet high. The building rested on a rock foundation that was over two feet high at the front of the building; and three steps about six feet in length, made of 2- to 10-inch boards, with a rise of perhaps eight inches, provided access to the door.

On the south side of South Pass Avenue, at the upper end of the street, is a log barn which was utilized by the mail and stage contractors to house their horses used in conveying the mail. It may have had other uses prior to this of which I have no definite knowledge, but was used as a stable after the destruction by fire of the barn. The remaining buildings on this side of the street were gone before my time, with the exception of a building which was probably built in the early nineties for a school. It was located a short distance west and south, on the south side of South Pass Avenue from the Freund building, and was about fifty feet from the street with the door facing to the east, and the building parallel to the street. This building was the last building used in South Pass as a school, and was built for and used exclusively as a school building. It was moved to its present location on the hill north of Custer Avenue between Washington and Jefferson streets. Moving consisted of tearing the building down, after marking the logs, then replacing them in the original order for the reconstructed building. This was done by a carpenter named Ed Walsh, of whom I may tell you more later. A couple of series of logs were added to give the building additional height.

It was in this building, when it was in the South Pass Avenue location, that I received my initiation into the mysteries of education, and I must have been quite a trial to those patient and wonderful teachers. I experienced great difficulty in grasping the true purpose of these tutors and took the first-grade work three times before it sunk in. However, with such a good start, I managed to catch up to the normal grade and age level by the time I reached fifth grade.

Some lessons were so deeply impressed upon my mind that I will never forget them. The school did not have a private "Chic Sales" toilet until later, so it was necessary to utilize the facilities of the Converse house (then occupied by the Bates family) across the street. In attending to nature's duties, my pocket knife slipped out of my pocket and fell through the hole. Now any red-blooded six-year-old boy of those days needed a jack knife, so it was necessary to retrieve this item. As I failed to return to the school building in a reasonable length of time, the teacher sent one of the older pupils, my cousin Billy Carr, to see why I was delayed. He found me vainly searching in the mire for the knife and persuaded me to reluctantly abandon the futile search. He hoisted me out of the hole and upon my return to the school, the teacher could see that the aroma would be very detrimental to the scholastic environment, so I was sent home for renovation.

On another occasion, Fred Carr discovered the Van Horn girl refreshing herself with a few sucks on a neatly constructed sugar tit before recess was over, with the result that the cloth was torn in the ensuing struggle and the sugar scattered all over the floor.

East of this location were the remnants of a stone chimney and a scrap-iron pile where a wheelwright and blacksmith ran an establishment. This shop was gone before I remember, as were also the other buildings along the street to the intersection of C Street.

We will now go up C Street, as there are a few buildings and locations of interest about which I have some definite knowledge. C Street is on the east side of a mile-long gulch that runs into Willow Creek from the north. There is a spring close to the head of this gulch, but the water is sometimes entirely absorbed by the earth in the fall of the year (as it is not a large spring) but it surfaces a little farther down the gulch, and from there there is usually some water in the stream all the way to Willow Creek. This spring was the source of water for domestic use for the residents on C Street. The gulch was called Mormon Gulch, but as there were no more Mormons living in this area than in other parts of the town, I do not know why it was given the name.

The house at the head of C Street was owned by a bachelor, John Bane, who passed away in February 1975. Formerly it was owned by "Baldy" Williams (E.J. Williams) who came to this section in the earlier days, and had business and mining interests. He later located at a now extinct town known as Elkhorn, on Big Sandy Stream, where he had a store and sawmill and where he was postmaster. He later moved to Rock Springs and secured employment as janitor at the Rock Springs National Bank. Some of his relatives now live in Lander.

There were a number of houses on the hillside and in the gulch in this vicinity, but the log house now owned by Mrs. Peter Marrin, located on the west side of C Street, is a house that was built by John Bane after a disastrous fire completely destroyed the previous house and all the possessions of Peter Marrin's parents, J.J. (Bob) Marrin and Nettie Marrin. The fire started from a faulty flue and burned in the ceiling; and with the limited flow of the spring behind the house, and the freezing temperatures, the fire gained such headway that there was no chance to salvage anything. The original house on this location was a log building but later had lumber additions and a covering of boards were placed vertically over the log portion, making it a very comfortable house.

Before Marrin's occupancy, the building was occupied by A.D. Shakspear, a practicing attorney in the mining camp. There is no knowledge as to any relationship to the English Bard, and there is a slight difference in the spelling of the name, as the e between the k and s is absent, as is also the final e. Shakspear was a charter member of Wyoming Lodge No. 28,

28

U.D. Grand Lodge of Nebraska, and was one of the committee appointed to draw up the original bylaws for this fraternity.

The next existing house on this side of the street is a two-story house that is now owned by heirs of James Earnest Smith. Earnest was my uncle, a child of a common mother and a stepfather of my father. I do not know who built or owned the house previously, but one of its occupants was a Colonel Ewing, who was a mining engineer, engaged by a mining company in the work of sampling the Carissa mine with a view toward purchase. Alvin Phillips was the mining engineer in charge of the mine, employed by John C. Spry, a Chicago lumber merchant, who was principal owner and president of the Federal Gold Mining Company.

It was Phillips' contention that a mill run was the only way to truly ascertain the true value of the ore, as the schist and diorite formations along the vein also carried values. In these mill tests, some high-grade ore had been stored in the shaft and workings, and an occasional load of this was secretly mixed with the practically barren rock. The mill-run tests were very satisfactory, but upon about the completion of the tests, the high-grade ore supply was exhausted and the values dropped, with the result that this clever scheme was apprehended by Col. Ewing. In his boisterous voice, augmented by his wrath, his names and opinions of the swindling engineer were heard by everybody on Carissa Hill and reverberated throughout the whole town.

Back of this house on the hillside was Dakota Street. This street was parallel to C Street and extended to the south side of town. West from the two-story house on the west side of Dakota Street, one sees a slight depression where a dugout in the hill was once the site of the Pioneer Brewery and Saloon, of which Engelbrecht and Nickschwitz were the proprietors.

On the north side was a tunnel a short distance back in the hill. I remember when this tunnel was well timbered, as it was not back to solid formation except on the floor at the back, where a small spring of very good, clear, cool water bubbled out of the rock and flowed out the tunnel. This was probably the water used in the brewing. It was reported as being a very good quality of beer. As evidence of the location is being gradually obliterated, it will not be long before it will be impossible to establish where this brewery was, unless it is suitably marked.

The next house now standing is presently owned by Mrs. Chipp of Rock Springs. She usually spends some time in the summer here. Fifty years ago, its occupants were two bachelors, Brigham Young Barrows and Frank Barrett. Frank Barrett was employed at the Carissa mine and fired the boilers that furnished the steam power for the machinery operating the mine and mill. In the later years of his employment, the operations consisted mainly of pumping the water out of the mine, as there was no ore production then. He had a full beard of a bluish-gray color and a very fine texture, with pleasing waves, that reached well down on his bosom over halfway to the waist. His soft blue eyes always held a fascinating twinkle that made them pleasingly attractive.

He suffered a severe stroke that left one side paralyzed, so he was unable to talk and could only take liquid nourishment. In about ten days, he passed away. He had no close relatives in this part of the country. Ed Walsh, the carpenter who lived in South Pass, made a suitable wooden coffin from the best lumber available, and my brother and I worked hard for two days to dig the grave. The ground was frozen the entire six feet, and the point of the pick could be driven in only about two and a half or three inches, and then only a small chip could be pried loose. His grave deserves a better marker than the small plain stone that was placed at the head of the grave, and which has probably disappeared by now.

Brigham Young Barrows worked at mining, and in his later years would spend the winters in Utah. He had a sister living in the east, and her finances would not permit her coming to Wyoming for the funeral. He was buried in the Lander cemetery.

The cabin that these bachelors occupied is a very old one and may have been constructed by the discoverers of the

Carissa Lode when they returned after the Indian episode.

It was somewhere back of this cabin, probably on Dakota Street, where Phillip Harsch had his blacksmith shop, the first blacksmith shop in South Pass City. He later moved to Atlantic City and had a shop there, which was operated after his death by a son, Henry. Henry Harsch was known in the region as Doggie Harsch, as he had a few head of cattle.

The next house now standing is presently owned by Raino Matson of Rock Springs, who usually spends some time each summer here. One of the former occupants was Dan Carmody, who worked for years at the Carissa mine. Dan had the reputation of being one of the most efficient men to work on the grizzley (an iron grate that separated the coarser ore, which was then broken into smaller pieces with a sledgehammer so that it was ready to go into the ore bins after passing through the crusher. These bins fed the ore into the stamp battery boxes). Carmody was the man previously mentioned in the

B. Y. Barrows cabin first house on left. Rock house used as first jail — by telephone pole. First house on right.

drilling contest. He was a cousin of John Carmody, an early stock man associated in the stock business with Noble and Lane, bankers in Lander, Wyoming. Dan was a bachelor, very bighearted, jovial, and his own worst enemy. He would take a vacation about once a year and would go to Lander and imbibe, occasionally in excess. He had a diamond ring valued at about five hundred dollars, which he usually sported on these sprees. He was a fellow who enjoyed company and would quite often buy drinks for all the occupants in the bar.

On one of these trips, he returned home with notches cut in the ring where some of his friends(?) had tried to cut the band, but were evidently disturbed in their work and did not get the job done. The ring fit too tightly for easy removal, so they had apparently adopted this method but been foiled in the attempt.

After the mine closed down, Dan went to live with his sister in San Francisco, where he remained for several years and where he disappeared. Some months after his disappearance, his body was found floating in the Bay. I would presume the ring played a part in his fate.

There are no more buildings on this side of C Street today. There are several buildings on the other side of the street, but the only one of particular interest is the rock structure across from the cabin that the Matsons own; it was used as the first jail in South Pass City. It was constructed of flat schist rock, and the prisoners were able to remove enough rock in the side of the wall to escape.

Other buildings lined the street to its junction with South Pass Avenue, but they have been gone as long as I can remember. However, a general merchandise store known as the store with the red front was located either on C Street or South Pass Avenue in this end of town, according to information from my grandmother. It was one of the more important establishments in the town and it could have been somewhere in this locality. C Street continued across Willow Creek to Smith Street (Grant Street).

CHAPTER

III

We will now go along South Pass Avenue, to the buildings occupying the lot on the northeast corner of the C Street and South Pass Avenue intersection. Facing on South Pass Avenue is a log building on a rock foundation that was built for community use for dances, meetings, and the like by Will Sherlock (my uncle) and George Flick, probably in the early 1890s. Before that there was probably a different building there, but I have no knowledge of it. George Flick was a very good mill operator employed at the Carissa mine. My uncle worked on another shift on this operation and was one of the best operators that ever worked with George on any mill he ever operated, according to Flick's appraisal. A certain amount of skill is required to feed the ore properly from the storage bins to the stamp battery boxes, maintaining proper mercury level in the troughs to amalgamate and to collect amalgam on the copper plates, in the gold-recovery process. When the mercury-gold amalgam is removed from the plates, a certain amount must be kept on the upper end of the plates so that future feedings will properly form in the new coating. If this is not done, the values will wash over the plates and go out with the tailings, and the values will be lost.

George Flick later left South Pass City, and with a man named Billie Halter, established a store, post office, saloon and road ranch at a spring on the head of Pacific Creek, which they called Pacific Springs. This operation was a profitable venture for Halter and Flick, but after sheep operations were established in the ranges around Pacific Springs, the herders would sometimes engage in drinking, gambling, wine and women, to the detriment of the livestock interests. So a purchase by the Blair and Hay Land and Livestock Company was negotiated, and these facilities were discontinued, converting to ranching operations only.

My uncle, the other partner in this building, was later associated with others in the family in the Smith-Sherlock Company store and the South Pass Land and Livestock operations. I recall a Christmas program put on by the school in this building when Alma Stork was the teacher. A portion of the back was curtained off for the performers, and a Christmas tree was placed on either side in front of the curtains that extended to the ceiling.

I also recall another show that was put on in this building, in the early 1900s. Two men came to town to stage a show and booked this hall. They sold quite a few tickets to their show, which was for adults only. A stage was curtained off in the back of the hall, and the benches for the seating were arranged with an aisle in the center down to the double-door entry. At last the night of the show listed on the billboard arrived, and a breathless audience anxiously awaited the drawing of the curtains, to see the show, *The Naked Shame*. The curtains were drawn and from the wings appeared a man in the nude with a lighted candle inserted in his rectum. He walked across the stage, then down the aisle and out the door. After this introduction the audience awaited the main show, but when no further action developed, it became clear that this introduction constituted the whole show. They began to look for the brazen actor who had perpetrated this fraud.

There were the tracks of two horses out in the street, where the actor and his accomplice had left town in great haste, under cover of darkness, and eluded the irate townsmen that followed in pursuit. I believe this was the only fraud that was ever pulled in this hall. Many of the old-time dances—square, round, quadrille, polka, schottische, Virginia reel, waltz, and two-step—were enjoyed in this log building, which was heated by a cast-iron box stove in the corner, from wood fuel. The walls and ceiling had a muslin lining, and although the building was well daubed, the two large windows and double doors in the front let in quite a bit of cold. There were not many wallflowers, as action was necessary to maintain body warmth and comfort. These dances usually lasted until daybreak, and a good time was had by all. On occasion, box suppers were raffled off, and a large coffeepot remained on the stove most of the time.

The native lumber floor did not wear very evenly as the knots were of harder substance and left humps when the softer wood wore away, but with proper waxing and a gradual rounding of the edge of the knots, the dancers' feet were able to gracefully glide over the floor as they tripped the light fantastic.

We will now journey down the street to the next door.

The next lot was occupied by a retail and wholesale liquor store. (There were two wholesale liquor stores in South Pass City, but I do not know where the other was located.) As this is on South Pass Avenue, I believe it was the 49'er, which carries the advertisement in the *Sweetwater Mines* by Billy Wilson that he is receiving the largest and best assortment of stock of wines, liquors, cigars, bar fixtures, etc., that ever came over the U.P.R.R. for this western country. The advertisement also states that after an experience of twenty years in the mines, he differs in opinion with some people that anything will do for a mining camp, as he knows as an old timer, that nothing but the very choicest and best is saleable to the miner. The advertisement also states that in the rear of the wholesale department there is a sample room under the supervision of G.W. Odell, professor of mixology, where samples can be tested. The establishment also claims to be sole agent for Willow Run, B. Marshal's Old Kentucky Bourbon, Keller's, Chicken Cock, Crow, McGee and Eldorado, Signette, and domestic brandy,

Holland gin, and port and sherry wines. Also a large invoice of choice brands of champagne. Agency for Iller & Co's, American Life Bitters and Rocky Mountain Cream Ale. This advertisement, which is a full column the length of the paper, claims that the restaurant is under the supervision of that well-known caterer to the public on the Pacific Coast for the last nineteen years, Captain Sherlock, and that Mrs. S. will at all times be ready to wait on her friends and try to make them comfortable by means of as square a meal as can be got in the city. Arrangements have been made both in Omaha and Salt Lake City for vegetables and every variety in the markets. Refreshments at all hours. Open all night. Particular attention is called to the sleeping apartment under the supervision of Mrs. S., which is sufficient guarantee that the greatly desired room is at last found in the camp, a good soft bed. This building was gone, perhaps before I was born, so I can only surmise that it was a two-story structure with the sleeping quarters over the restaurant and bar. The wholesale liquor warehouse was dug back into the hill, and the walls were well rocked up with the flat rock so well suited for this purpose. It was a very substantial and skilled, workmanlike job. The front wall dividing this part from the front part was also made of stone about thirty inches thick, with a door of quarter-inch sheet iron, a little less than six feet high and thirty-two or more inches wide. Hinges were of the same quarter-inch strap iron two inches wide, riveted to the door, the ends constructed so that a three-quarter inch pin would fit into the hole made by bending the two-inch strip to form a complete loop. This pin was made by bending the rod at right angles so that the two-inch pin would turn up; the other part would extend back some distance into the wall and was incorporated in its construction. There was a hinge at the top, center and bottom. The door was installed before the capstone was placed over it. Thus it was impossible to remove the door after installation without major destruction to the wall. The capstone over the door was a rock at least twelve inches thick, sixteen inches across, and about five feet long. The door had a slot about six inches long by two inches high cut into it about three fourths of the way up; an iron slide allowed opening or closing the hole. The door was fastened with a one-inch bolt that would slide in the supporting brackets riveted in place, like the operation of what is known as a barrel bolt. A piece of flat iron was welded to this bolt, which had a slot in it that would fit over an eye bolt, which would then allow a padlock to be used to lock the door. The room was perhaps sixteen by twenty feet. The roof was made of heavy log stringers, over which poles were placed, and the latter covered with a good covering of rock and dirt. This was the back room of the building, and although the door was taken quite a while ago, the walls back in the hill dugout were in fair shape until Fremont County undertook improvements on the road, and in the relocation, this landmark was destroyed. The Captain Sherlock mentioned in the advertisement was no relation as far as I know. A Captain Sherlock was discharged from the service at the end of his enlistment, from Fort Leavenworth I believe, some years before and was probably the person referred to.

The next house on the street was a house used as a residence. I remember it as a two-room house with a lumber front but with sides and back of logs. There was a double-sash window on the west side of the door in front and a window in the back room on the east side of the building. A door in the back opened into a lean-to shed made of lumber with slabs to batten the cracks. The roof was made of boards, but the roof of the house was of shingles. The lining was the customary muslin covered with wallpaper. A covered porch ran the full width of the front of the house, with a wooden railing enclosure about two feet high except at the entrance. One of the occupants of this house was a doctor, Dr. Lovejoy, one of two Lovejoys, brothers, in South Pass City, Doc and Fred. Fred later went to Jackson, Wyoming, where he managed the early telephone operations. It was while Dr. Lovejoy lived in this house that he performed an operation on Dave Tweed.

William (Boss) Tweed had moved his family to the head of Red Canyon, where he took up ranching and farming. Some soldiers were dispatched to Ft. Stambaugh, and as they came to the Tweed ranch and did not know the country, they solicited the services of Dave, a boy of about fifteen, to guide them to the fort. The trip to the fort was uneventful, but on the return trip, a storm from the northeast blew up and Dave was caught out and spent the night in the blizzard. His feet were badly frozen. He was taken to South Pass City, and it was in this house that Dr. Lovejoy amputated the toes, ball of the foot, and portion of the instep. As whiskey was the only anesthesia, which was very inadequate for the ordeal, the boy's agonized cries were audible throughout the town. Special handmade boots were required for him after he was able to walk again. I remember that the leather boots housed only about a three- or four-inch foot, but Dave walked in a very credible manner, and at one time operated a taxi service in the town of Lander. Some of Dave's relatives still live in Lander today. Dave spent quite a bit of his time in the Fremont Hotel lobby or the pool hall, where he could be called for taxi service, and was a very familiar figure on the streets of Lander. He was a fairly good weather prognosticator, but on rare occasions, his forecasts were in error and his fellowmen enjoyed emphasizing the fact. They would ask Dave, "What happened to that storm you predicted?" To which Dave would answer, "Well, by gum, it sure snowed somewhere." Who could truthfully say he was wrong?

I believe it was when Dr. Lovejoy left that Jim Smith acquired this house, and it became known to my father and uncle as the Jim Smith House. As constable or marshal, Jim Smith was engaged in upholding the law and order of the community. The Local Matters column carries the item, in the June 19, 1869, issue of the *Sweetwater Mines*, "Our worthy Marshal, Jas. Smith, is doing much toward keeping down such persons as are disposed to violate the town ordinances." Also in this issue is an item about the arrangements for the celebration for the Fourth of July. The citizens of South Pass held a meeting, and a committee of five, consisting of W.C. Ervin, Lem Colbath, E.A. Slack, Judge Strunk and Major Baldwin were appointed and authorized to make arrangements for the celebration of our National Independence. Judge Strunk was chosen chairman and G.W. Wardman was appointed secretary. On motion, it was unanimously resolved that James Smith, Esq., be requested to act as marshal of the day. On motion, a cordial invitation was directed to be extended to the Atlantic and Hamilton cities, to the residents of the entire Sweetwater Mining District and the Wind River Valley to join with South Pass City in the celebration of this anniversary of the first important event in the history of the United States.

The next lot was the site of a house that was constructed of logs sawed in half—for the sides and back—and of shiplap for the square false front. The front porch constituted part of the board sidewalk along the street. The occupant of this house was a man of Greek origin, Antone Stubo by name. He was a man of small stature and rather lean, unlike most of his race that I have known, who quite often engage in catering to the public in restaurants of which they are the proprietors. Antone's mine was a shaft on the north side of the present road into South Pass, not over a quarter of a mile from the brass cap marking the quarter corner between sections seventeen and eighteen. It never produced a great amount of ore.

Antone also had some horses which grazed on pastures and hills southwest of South Pass City, at the head of Dead Ox Gulch. This gulch was called Dead Ox because an ox once died there. Poison baits placed there by a trapper netted over forty red-fox pelts and one cross-fox pelt. The pasture, which was called Antone's Pasture, was fenced with poles nailed to posts fastened together to form an X, which is known as a buck fence. In a small grove of trees at the head of the northeast branch of this gulch were the remains of two rock fireplaces, where early day cabins once stood. I would surmise that they were erected by the early hunters and trappers before South Pass City was established. I believe reference has been made to their existence in some early writings, designating them as the "Burns," and they were probably destroyed by fire, as there is some charcoal on the location as well as among the trees.

Antone had some very good draft stock among his horses,

and he would make occasional sales, thus furnishing a living for his frugal way of life. On one occasion, he had the misfortune to have a fire in his house, and he hurriedly removed a tin tea-kettle, a dishpan and a saucepan across the street, where they would be safe from any consuming flames. Neighbors came to his rescue and extinguished the flames before they could do any major damage.

I have wondered why he did not try to remove his violin. It was a very old and sweet-toned instrument, which was later sold by J.J. Marrin to an engineer who was in South Pass taking samples from Carissa mine with a view toward a possible purchase. Antone owed Marrin and Moore a liquor bill at their saloon at the time of his demise, so the property was acquired for the debt. Marrin sold the logs in this house to my brother, who used them and another portion of the old Carr building to make a garage for his car on the former location of the Baskin and DeWolf assay office.

Cattle herds were trailed along through the South Pass on the Oregon Trail to the Oregon and Montana ranges, and men would frequently stop on the Sweetwater to rest their horses and weary herds. The cowboys would refresh themselves by coming to South Pass City a short distance to the north of this trail, as it was the largest city between Denver and Salt Lake City. It was on one of these visitations that Antone Stubo was walking down the north side of the street when one of the cowboys emerged from the saloon and called to him to come over and have a drink. At that time the bar was owned by Jim Smith, with whom Antone had probably had troubles, and there was considerable bad blood between the two men. Antone replied, "I do not drink in that S— of-a-B— bar." The cowboy considered this refusal to his hospitality as a grave insult and started after Antone, who ran. The cowboy grabbed a rock and threw it at Antone, striking and knocking him down. Antone was running toward the hill to get behind some buildings, but he fell near a building that had been destroyed by fire. Grasping a charred two-by-four beam, Antone managed to land a blow that floored the inebriated cowboy. The cowboy's partners, watching from the saloon, were infuriated and entered into hot pursuit of Antone, who ran down the street and into the front door of a house just east of the courthouse. There was one small window with a hinged sash with two ten-by-twelve-inch glass panes in a small pantry and storage room at the back of the house. Antone, being small, managed to escape through this window and fled among the buildings, into the Hermit, a small stream that runs into Willow Creek east of South Pass City. Here he remained in hiding for two days until the cowboys returned to their trail herd, thus averting what would most certainly have been a lynching by this intoxicated bunch. Antone's animosity was limited to Jim Smith only, as very friendly relations always existed between him and all the other members of the family.

Across the street from Antone's house is a small spring that has caused a washing and eroding of the ground into Willow Creek, so that a rock retaining wall was built. It was here that Antone had a small garden.

I do not know what building occupied the next site. It was gone before I can remember. The next lot was the site of a small log building. The logs were notched with the builder's axe, and the ends not very even. A stone fireplace in the center of the back wall furnished the heat. The roof was made of log stringers covered with poles and a liberal coat of rock and dirt, with very little pitch. It was a low building, its walls only about six or six and a half feet high, and a man of medium height had to use care in entering. The floor space did not exceed twelve by fourteen feet, and I do not believe it was even that large. The rocks where the fireplace was constructed are still visible. This cabin had a dirt floor, and the bare logs on the inside lacked the usual muslin lining. It was the first building used as a schoolhouse in South Pass City. A couple of wooden benches constituted the seating and the desks were the space under the bench where the slate and slate pencil and a few textbooks were neatly placed. There were five or six pupils in this school, among whom were my uncle, Peter Sherlock, Dave Tweed, and Willie Steers. The teacher was Old

Man Stillman, (J.W. Stillman, justice of the peace, who resigned when the woman suffrage bill was approved by the Wyoming Territorial Legislature). The teacher's salary consisted of food or any article that could be used in the course of living, in some instances room and board with the pupils' parents for a specified length of time, along with what money could be provided by the children's parents. Eventually the legislature met and appropriated funds for payment of a salary out of tax collections. Later, more elaborate desks were made by the parents, who were responsible for upkeep and repairs of same. The number of pupils also increased.

The next house now standing is a two-room log cabin with a shed built on the back. It was a residence, although it was in this house that my brothers and I went to school several months after an altercation erupted that forced the regular school to close, and my father arranged for the teacher to continue the tutelage of the pupils in our family. (This was about sixty years ago.) The building now belongs to James and Janet Tibbals, whose father was mining engineer at the Carissa mine when he acquired the property.

Across the street, one lot east, is a spring where my grandfather had a bathhouse. When Richard Sherlock, came to the South Pass Country in the spring of 1868, he paid $700 for a ferry that operated on the Sweetwater about a mile below the present crossing of the stream by State Highway No. 28. This was also the location of the county road before the new highway was built; it is also where Dave Dickie of the L.U. Sheep Company (now in Thermopolis country) built dipping vats to treat his flocks to rid them of ticks, when he ranged his sheep in this section. When the ferry proved unprofitable, Sherlock moved his family to South Pass, and I believe it was about this time that he built the bathhouse. The bathhouse was a small two-story structure, where the water from the spring was pumped and heated in the upper story. There were two tubs, one upstairs and one on the ground floor, one metal and one wooden. This venture was more profitable (with baths at fifty cents) but could not provide for the needs of a growing family, and grandfather engaged in other employment. He was working in a sawmill up on Willow Creek when he contracted pneumonia and died.

In later years, the water from this spring was piped down to a wooden barrel tub under the floor of the kitchen in the Sherlock hotel, and a hand pump was installed. This became the source of water for the hotel.

The next house east of the bathhouse is a two-room log house in which the Wyoming Historical Commission shows a very interesting narrated slide program at designated times for the information and entertainment of visitors. At the time the Sherlock family came to South Pass City, Mrs. Tweed, the first white woman to settle in the town, Mrs. Kime, later Mrs. Chapin, and possibly Mrs. Ramsey lived in the town. Mrs. Kime operated a boardinghouse in this building. I later knew it as the Leckie House, as a family by that name lived in it. Sam Leckie was the only fatal accident victim I know of in the Carissa mine. While walking along the drift tunnel, in the dim light of his miner's candle, he failed to see that the trapdoor covering the shaft to the lower levels was not closed, and he fell down the shaft. He and some other members of the family are buried in the cemetery on the hill south of South Pass City.

My uncle, Wm. Carr, ran a butcher shop in this building a short while. Near the front of the building was a spring. A log crib about three feet high was built around it. It was so close to the street intersection that it was almost impossible for a string team with two wagons to negotiate the turn without damage to the crib curbing, so Ed Walsh, a carpenter and millwright resident, removed the curb and buried a pipe from the spring to the edge of Willow Creek, to carry the water. The spring is so pure and cold that a person has to drink it slowly, and it does not quench the thirst any better than distilled water. Within my memory, this spring went dry only twice, after very light winters in the mountains, and failed to run for a period of about two weeks. On the last occasion, one fall, we had a storm on the mountain that reached only to Highway 28. There was no precipitation east of the highway, although considerable moisture west of it. After this storm, the spring began to flow again, so it is undoubtedly fed from a fissure that extends some distance into the mountain.

Back to the north side of South Pass Avenue, we find the Carissa Saloon. It may have had another name earlier, but this was its name when I remember it and it was owned by Marrin and Moore. While patronizing this establishment, Billy Carr imbibed somewhat in excess, and when the wife sent one of the children down to tell him to come home, he had the child return to deliver the message that he was too drunk to come home and if she wanted him to return home, they would have to come after him with the wheelbarrow. This they did. This building was a log building with the square-frame lumber front. The front corner of the building was damaged considerably when struck by a bulldozer that was not properly controlled by an operator when the railroad to the iron mine over on

South Pass Avenue, West of the Price Street intersection.
Notice well curbing at left.

Rock Creek was being built.

The next building east of the Carissa saloon and on South Pass Avenue where Price Street ends, was a frame building called the White Swan, high in front but only one in the back store room which was dug back into the hill and the walls of well laid rock. The entrance to the top story of the frame building was a stairway up the hill to the roof of the store room and through a door in the back of the building from the roof. The front of this building was of the square type, with boards placed vertically and the joints battened with four-inch boards. As I remember this building, it had a four-foot wainscoating, with wallpapered muslin above the wainscoating. The ceiling was of painted boards. It was operated as a restaurant, saloon and gambling house. The upstairs consisted of a small dance hall and rooms where women of loose morals plied their trade.

CHAPTER

IV

We now come to the Smith-Sherlock store building. This building is made up of two separate buildings. The new part was probably about twenty feet from the White Swan and was built in 1897 or 1898. There may have been a building on this site prior to that, but if so, I do not know what it was.

This building's sides and back are constructed of logs with a square frame shiplap front. The ends of the logs in this building, like most of the buildings with frame fronts, were cut with a two-inch tongue and were spiked in a channel made by nailing two-by-two lumber to a squared eight-by-eight timber.

Although this mode of construction was perhaps not as substantial as the notched-log technique, it would give many years of service. This part of the building was lined with what was termed compo-board, no longer manufactured. It was made like our present plasterboard, except that the core was of four-foot strips of lath, three-fourths of an inch wide and one-eighth inch thick, placed on a cardboard base and embedded in a fine sand-and-lime plaster, to which a top layer of cardboard was placed, making a four-by-eight-foot, quarter-inch-thick sheet of board, resembling our present-day plasterboard.

The logs in this building were used in the construction of an Episcopal church in South Pass. A few more logs were added to give the building additional height.

Perhaps it would be well to explain here why the church approved the sale of the logs. The gold-rush boom days of South Pass City were over by the late nineties, and as the building was used infrequently, it required upkeep which it would not receive. It was deemed advisable to dispose of it while it had some value, especially when it could be utilized to advantage by a party willing to purchase it. Through the Rev. Roberts, negotiations were entered into and the sale consummated. There was a partition across the back of the building, back of which another partition about seven feet high and at right angles divided this room into two rooms. There was a window in the west room of this back room, which was used as a post office and telephone exchange. In the east room was a doorway that led into the old building, which was about eight feet from this newer part of the store. A hallway about six feet wide connected the two buildings. Some of the stock was kept in the east room, which was also used as a bedroom for many years by my blind uncle, Peter. A brick chimney was incorporated in the main partition, and the store building was heated by a large cast-iron stove known as a box stove. It was centrally located in the building, and a horizontal six-inch stovepipe of about seven or eight joints, each two feet in length, conducted the smoke to the chimney from the vertical pipe from the stove. This stove could use blocks of wood up to twenty-eight to thirty inches long and was a very efficient source of heat for the establishment. The length of the overhead pipe acted somewhat as a heat combustion chamber, which also added to the efficiency of the stove.

The ceiling was made of beaded boards, and a shingled roof over a sheeting of native lumber covered the building. Two counters in front of the shelving on either side of the building had passageways between the counters and at the north ends. These four counters had two-inch redwood tops, over which a large variety of merchandise passed, since this was the only general store to operate in the later years. One side of the store was given to food items, while the other was mostly clothing, jewelry and notions. Hardware for the most

Smith-Sherlock Company Store. Old Colter & Houghton
section at right.

At store entrance: Donald Sherlock, John Sherlock, and
Peter Sherlock.

First customer at the door, Smith-Sherlock Store.

Smith-Sherlock Store porch, Christmas, 1927.

part was kept in the storerooms and warehouse. The old-fashioned coffee mill, which was used to grind the roasted coffee beans, was located on the north end of the counter on the grocery, or east side, and a small section on the south end of the south counter was latticed off where the day book and customer ledger were kept. The customer ledger was a large, serviceable leather-bound ledger about four inches thick. Twelve-by-sixteen inch pages neatly reflected each transaction itemized in the day book. The glass window pane in the right front door as you entered the building was broken out by two burglars. The crash of the glass and their voices awakened my blind uncle in his bedroom, and he asked what they wanted. He was told to get back in bed and he would not be hurt. He had to do as ordered, closing the door and remaining in his bedroom. The cash register in those days consisted of a drawer mounted under the counter with several pull lugs, which when properly pulled, would disengage the locking device and allow opening of the drawer. This drawer was pried off, and with a little tobacco and a few cans of food, the robbers departed. The cash drawer was found a few days later behind a barn on the south side of Grant (Smith) Street at the Price Street intersection. The checks and papers were scattered around but were retrieved, and so the monetary loss was minimal. More than a year later a customer came into the store, and in conversation, asked my father if they had ever found out who robbed the store. After he left, Uncle Peter inquired who the man was and told father that this was one of the men who had robbed the store. Thinking back, they recalled that two men were around South Pass at the time of the robbery and left just afterward. Thus they were identified by the sound of one man's voice. As losses were small and of no consequence, nothing was done about it.

There was another attempted robbery in the 1920s. The incident happened late in the fall. It was customary for employees to close the store around eight o'clock and go to the hotel, as there was not much business after that hour. A young man, Ed Hayden, had been employed during the summer and fall, and as he left the store just prior to closing, he saw a man run around the old part of the building, so he went back and reported to my father. They looked around and did not find anyone, so they proceeded to close the store and go on to the hotel. Hayden went out the back door and over the stream to the corral, where he could see part of the store. Looking at the store in the semidarkness, he thought he could see a man at the window in the back room where the postoffice was located. The man evidently saw Hayden also, as he disappeared behind the building. This window was covered by a wooden shutter fastened from the inside by raising the sash and fastening the hook. Hayden reported what he had seen to father, who stayed in the front office of the hotel building while the balance of the family were in the dining room. Hayden then resumed his station in the yard. The burglar evidently decided it would be best to scout around, and before long he crawled on the front porch of the hotel and peeked through the window. My father ordered him to stop or he would shoot. The man started to run, and the shot struck him in the upper leg. He said "You got me," and surrendered. The sheriff in Lander was notified, and the burglar placed under guard on a couch. The sheriff took him to the jail in Lander. His wound was just a flesh wound. There was a bag of tools by the window where he had been trying to pry the shutter open. The car he had parked up the street was well loaded with merchandise, mostly clothing that he had obtained from several other robberies, and charges were filed against him by the rightful owners. These were the only two robberies experienced by this store.

The old portion of the store built by Colter and Houghton was the first store in South Pass City. The back was built of flat schist rock, as were the sides and front up to about four and a half feet, where boards were nailed vertically to the timbers and the cracks battened with boards to complete the walls in this portion of the building. There were two rooms, each with a front window made with a single sash of six panes of ten-by-twelve-inch glass. These windows were protected by one and a half inch strap-iron grills bolted over the windows.

The original roof was of poles covering the stringers, and these were covered with dirt. The inner lining of muslin periodically received a coating of Kalsomine. The business office consisted of a southwest corner in the west room of the building. The post office was also there until moved to the new addition. After the erection of the new building, this portion was used as a warehouse and was a museum project of the South Pass Restoration program of the State of Wyoming.

The next building on this side of the street was destroyed by fire, as were the remaining buildings to the corner of Washington Street. This section of town experienced two disastrous fires. The next site was occupied by the Kidder Hotel, the only three-story building in the town to the best of my knowledge. It was a two-by-four stick in the rubble of this building that Antone Stubo used on the cowboy who was chasing him, as previously related. The hotel stood at a slight angle to South Pass Avenue. Excavation here reveals some of the charcoal from the fires.

A dugout in the hill is located behind these buildings. It probably survived the fires because of its rock structure, and was later used by Smith-Sherlock Company as a storeroom for the saloon liquors and the store supplies. The dugout was divided into two rooms; the partition had an iron door with hinges extending into the walls. The barrel bolt could be locked by the flat strap iron which was welded to the inch bolt and had a slot that fit over the eye bolt riveted to the door. The padlock was then locked in the eye blot. This door was of perhaps three-eighths sheet metal, a boxlike structure, fabricated so that welding at the corner and ends and where the completed sides met at the back of the completed door formed a hollow door about five or six inches thick.

The ceiling was of hewn timbers fitted tightly together, on which about eighteen inches of dirt was placed; on top of this was the roof, with probably about one-fourth pitch, made of boards crosswise to the building, and boards over the joints, thus allowing most of the melting snow and rain to drain off. The front room of this building was about half inside the hill and did not have the ceiling but had the roof, as in the back. The room was not built for warmth, and the merchandise stored here could not be harmed by cold: wagon hardware (spokes, fellies, tongues, etc.), Norwegian drill steel, kerosene, and in the early days of the automobile, fifty-gallon drums of gasoline. The gasoline was measured out in a gallon measure and placed in a five-gallon can, and from this it was poured into the gas tank of the automobile. The back room made an excellent cellar, and potatoes could be stored in the bin and would not sprout until the first of June, and with a little sprouting, would remain palatable until the fourth of July. Vinegar was kept here in a fifty-gallon barrel that had a wooden spigot, and the customer brought his jug to be filled. It was the store room for canned fruits, vegetables, and milk, as it was necessary to store enough winter supplies to last until the roads opened in the spring. Sometimes, as much as a car-load of milk was stored here in the fall of the year.

A box containing some quart bottles of peppermint extract used for mixing drinks and some silver-and-gold-label imported champagne remained stored in this part of the building several years after the saloon closed. My older brother knew about them, and I remember on one occasion we secretly took two bottles of the champagne with us on a swimming party. There were about six of us in the party, and going down Willow Creek, below town, we had a wonderful time swimming by a beaver dam. The water was always rather chilly, even in mid-summer, but our childhood toughness would not allow for this. After the party we returned home, but my younger brother and another boy about the same age became very sick. The mothers decided it was because we had gone swimming in the cold water too soon after eating dinner, but I am inclined to believe the champagne was the real cause of their troubles. We used more care in the consumption of champagne after that.

The Indians stole the horses of the townspeople a couple of times, but because of its population they never molested the town. A herder would take the horses out in the morning and herd them in the hills around the town and bring them back in the evening. On one or two occasions, the Indians came to the top of the hill and shot a few arrows into the town. About the turn of the century, a large band of Indians on the warpath passed through the country, pillaging and killing those who lacked the protection of numbers or were surprised. At that time the men of South Pass armed themselves and went hunting the Indians, leaving only a couple of the older men in South Pass to guard the women and children, who were gathered in the back room of the cellar. The population was vulnerable at that point, but the war party altered its course and was not encountered by the armed men from South Pass. A monument erected and dedicated by the organization that started the preservation of South Pass City is located in this part of town.

The next building, erected where some of the older buildings were burnt down, is presently utilized as living quarters for the supervisor and caretaker of the restoration project. Originally, it consisted of a two-room log building, but later another log addition was added to the east side. Still later, a well was dug, over which a frame addition was added on the north, serving as a kitchen, and a small shed was constructed at the back-door entry on the east side of the kitchen.

The birth of woman suffrage had something in common with my older brother and me. We were born in South Pass City on South Pass Avenue. This building, which then consisted of two rooms, was our birthplace, while woman suffrage can claim its origin farther down the street on the other side. This building was built by my father at the time of his marriage, with additions as the family increased in size. The well in this house is still used as a source of water in this part of town.

The next building that was torn down in the late nineteen twenties or early thirties, was a low log building that was used as a blacksmith shop. I do not know when it was built, but I remember the back door, which was of smooth lumber and located in the northeast corner of the building. Several brands and initials were burnt on the boards by hot irons; on the upper part the name of Geo. Ryder was burnt in letters about two and a half inches high. Ryder was employed as stage driver to carry mail and passengers on the South Pass—Bryan route. It was on a trip he was making with my aunt as a passenger when they were caught out in a blizzard in which he froze to death. Rev. Roberts, an Episcopal missionary on his way from England to the Indian Reservation was also on the incoming stage from Bryan, and was marooned at the Dry Sandy Station in this blizzard of 1883. Ryder was buried in a snowbank, and later, when spring came, the body was brought to the cemetery on the hill south of South Pass, and buried. It rests in an unmarked grave. One of the first entries in Rev. Roberts' church record is the notation of this burial. (I believe the Laramie church records are in Fort Washakie now.) They were in the Lander church at the time I saw them.

We are now at the intersection of Washington Street and South Pass Avenue. On the northeast corner stood the Sweetwater County Courthouse. When Wyoming became a territory in 1869, Sweetwater County extended from the Montana line on the north to Colorado on the south. Prior to this, South Pass City was in Carter County, Dakota Territory, and was prominently mentioned as a possible location for the state capital, but with the coming of the railroad and its surrounding settlements, Cheyenne was chosen.

The gold rush excitement subsided in South Pass after a few years, and the population exodus began. Some of the inhabitants went to lower elevations where the winters were not so severe—in the Wind River Valley, or along the U.P. Railroad. With this shift in population, candidates elected to fill the county offices were often residents of these growing communities. Travel conditions were bad and as the men were reluctant to move to the county seat, to make their residence, there was a widespread desire to move the county seat to a different location. After considerable controversy, some of the business of the county offices was moved to Green River. Rock Springs was thriving at this time and cast a covetous eye on the idea of locating the courthouse there. A courthouse was built which must have been financed by the city or some of its enterprising businessmen. The shufflings back and forth between South Pass City and Green River of the transactions, meetings, etc., must have caused a great deal of confusion. In the early spring of 1874, a couple of the county officers who resided in Green River came in a buckboard one night and loaded all the movable records into their rig and started for Green River. There were snowdrifts in the draws, and they would get stuck in these drifts on the road from time to time and would have to unload, get the rig across, carry the records across the drift and reload. In the course of these operations, it appears that many of the records were lost or destroyed to lighten the work of transporting them. Among these was probably a plat of the townsite of South Pass City as laid out in the early days, as there does not appear to be one in existence now, and many locations are referred to by lot and block number on a plat, in the deeds and records. I do not know if this vacillation over the location of the courthouse and county seat was the result of electors voice voting, but there were evidently three shifts of business and meetings, indicating that the opponents were fairly evenly divided. Eventually, a writ of mandamus was issued, and I presume the judge would not have issued this order unless the location of the county seat had been properly submitted to the qualified voters and the Green River location had received a majority of votes. This must have been prior to December 1873, as the writ designates when the county seat was moved. The old residents give the date of moving as 1874, and this date is marked in numbers five inches high on the door of one of the inside cells in the jail. I do not know what use was made of the building in Rock Springs, but the vote established the Green River location.

Recent construction of a new courthouse and county office building in Green River, truly a beautiful and magnificent building, has made provision for also housing a museum, under the able direction of Henry F. Chadey. There it was my privilege to read and reflect on the entries in the South Pass City courthouse records. There were about fifteen saloons, two wholesale liquor houses, and two breweries, and about the same number of general merchandise stores in South Pass City, most of which also dealt in liquor. These records show payment of numerous liquor license fees of one hundred or one hundred fifty dollars. I also noticed a great variation of the amount of surety on the required bonds for those filling public offices. To me, the surety seemed rather high, in view of the $18.75 per ounce price of gold and the purchasing power of the dollar in those days. F.W. Wisewell, a judge of probate court and *ex officio* county treasurer, was bonded in the amount of ten thousand dollars; Joseph F. Robinson and Harry Robinson were the sureties on this bond. John O'Donnell as county clerk was bonded for four thousand dollars.

The next building below the courthouse on South Pass Avenue was a low log building to which log additions were added. It consisted of five rooms plus a large woodshed, built in single file parallel to South Pass Avenue. In front of this building and across the board sidewalk, a distance of about fifteen feet, was a small building made of logs, probably eight by ten feet, which covered a well that furnished the water supply for the house. A rope secured to the framework was passed through a shiv wheel anchored to the ridge log in the roof and long enough to reach the bottom of the well; a bucket was tied to the end and this was used to draw up water by hand. It was in this well that a small mule belonging to one of the citizens of the town managed to fall when the door of the building was left open. It took about half of the male population of the town to get ropes on it and pull it out, however it did not appear to be much worse for the experience. After that, a solid board railing about three feet high was built around the well.

It was in the log building that the first white child was born in South Pass City, E.A. Amoretti. Mr. Amoretti became one of the prominent personalities in the history of the county and state, and was involved in agriculture, banking, livestock, and commercial activities in the county. This was also the building in which Antone Stubo eluded his pursuers in the incident previously related in our story, and it later became the home of John W. Bilcox, where he raised a large family. Bilcox was a veteran of the Civil War on the Union side. He lost practically all his eyesight, a loss attributed to moon-blindness caused by the moon's rays shining in his eyes as he slept in the open during his military duties. In later life, as the blindness became more advanced, he received a small pension from the federal government. He was scalped by the Indians and left for dead in one of his encounters, but recuperated, although completely bald as long as I can remember. The scar of the scalp removal operation was plainly visible. When the troops were stationed at Fort Stambaugh to protect the inhabitants of this vicinity from Indians, Bilcox and a partner secured a contract to furnish winter cordwood for the fort for one year. The specified cordage was stacked at the fort. A federal inspector happened to come to Stambaugh and in walking over the top of the woodpile, fell through into a hole that was neatly stacked in the corded wood. Closer inspection revealed many holes, with the result that Bilcox and his partner had to cut wood to fill the holes before the wood was accepted and the belligerent inspector pacified. The muslin lining removed from the Bilcox house after it was abandoned provided play tents for us which we erected in the willows below town for our games.

The next building I remember was a log building with the square-frame front and the sides made of two lengths of twenty-foot logs joined by an upright log mortise-and-tongue construction. This made a forty-foot room in the front part of the building. A log addition was built behind, but the corners were of dovetail construction. There were no side windows in the front portion, since the large window area in the front furnished sufficient light for the large room, its high ceiling ten feet or more. The back part of the building was not so large; however it had an upstairs and the ceiling of the first floor was not more than eight feet high. The upstairs part was divided into several rooms, but it was gutted and most of the flooring and partitions were removed. The stringers (floor sills) were logs that were hewn flat on two sides. This building was referred to as the Smith House by my father and uncle, but why, I

Smith House.

do not know. It was a hotel and may have been run by someone by the name of Smith.

Below this building was another small building that may have been used as a residence but was utilized as a chicken coop by the Bilcox family. Below this, there may have been a street. What looks like a road runs down the hill at about this point, from Custer Avenue across South Pass Avenue to Grant (Smith) Avenue. Below this, there is evidence of another large building, as considerable earth was moved from the hill to level the terrain. There is now a one-room cabin, which I believe was built by B.W. (Brick) Moore. Mr. Moore was associated with J.J. Marrin in the operation of the Carissa saloon. The cabin was probably built after other older buildings disappeared.

Jefferson Street ran from the Carissa Gulch down across Custer Avenue, South Pass Avenue, and Grant (Smith) Avenue, then up the hill south of town. There was another house between the Moore cabin and the intersection of Jefferson Street and South Pass Avenue, but it disappeared, probably before I was born.

On the northeast corner of the intersection was a log house with three rooms built parallel to South Pass Avenue, its entrance from the Avenue. There was a well between the walk and the Street, in front of the first room of the house. (A number of wells were dug on either side of South Pass Avenue because it was more convenient to secure water from a well than from the stream, especially in the winter.) I do not know who occupied this cabin first, but in the early nineteen hundreds, Mrs. S.F. Gillespie lived here. Her husband either died or left her, and a cousin, Ben Covey, lived with her. The relationship was questioned by some of the residents of the town. She had a daughter a few years older than I. Mrs. Gillespie had the mail contract between South Pass and Lander when she lived here, and Cousin Ben was a great help to her in carrying the mail. After leaving South Pass City, she lived around Lewiston, where she had staked out rather extensive copper claims. In a promotion deal, she endeavored to sell stock in

Kansas City and had quite a write-up in a Sunday edition of the *Kansas City Star*, referring to her as the Copper Queen, but I don't think she was too successful in this scheme, and I understand she operated a house of questionable repute.

There was another house or two that disappeared before I can remember, and the next house now standing is a log cabin which was occupied by a Civil War veteran in the early nineteen hundreds, a Mr. William Reiniker, who may have built it and occupied it from the early days. This cabin faced a street that merged in Carissa Gulch with Jefferson Street and carried the name of one of the presidents of the U.S., possibly Monroe or Pierce. The cabin had a pole-and-dirt roof but this has been replaced with another type roof and an addition has been built on the front. After Reiniker died, there were a great number of different occupants, and the Lander Business and Professional Women's Club was considering buying it and moving it across the street to make a replica of the first office and home of Esther Hobart Morris, as it was similar to her cabin. I have not heard of the outcome of this transaction. The cabin is now owned by Mrs. Zoie Lee of Rock Springs.

On the other side of this street on South Pass Avenue was another cabin of similar construction. However, the Reiniker cabin door faced east, and this cabin's door faced south on South Pass Avenue. The cabin was last occupied by J.M. Dumphrey, but was probably one of the earlier residences of the town. Dumphrey later homesteaded on the head of Fish Creek, about five miles southwest of South Pass City, and used the cabin on his occasional trips to town.

A barn stood across the street near the site of the former Esther Morris home, and this was used by Dumphrey to shelter his team while in town. Colin McPherson "Scottie" Spiers homesteaded on land adjacent to and south of Dumphrey. Dumphrey had a rather loudmouthed, bluffing nature, and when the Robert Jack Sheep Company ranged their sheep up to his fence, he would carry his gun and order the sheepherder, who was usually a man of Spanish-American extraction with little knowledge of English, to remove the flock from the vicinity. In response to his "no savvy" reply, Dumphrey said he could usually improve the comprehension greatly by hoisting the toe of his boot to the seat of the other's pants. Scottie was sometimes employed by the Jack Sheep Company when supplemental labor was required, and it was on one of these occasions that an altercation arose. As a result Scottie went to his home about half a mile distant, got his gun, returned and shot his neighbor. The body lay a few feet north of Dumphrey's north fence. Scottie was sentenced to a jail term and served several years before being pardoned. On a trip to town about a week before this killing, Dumphrey had picked up Scottie's mail to take it out to him, with the remark that there were worse people in the world than Scottie.

There were no buildings standing below the Carissa Gulch within my memory, although remains of several buildings can be found.

In the earlier days, this section of town was a swampy marshland, and beaver dams in Willow Creek aggravated the condition; but due to sluicing operations and tailings wash from later operations of the Carissa Mine, the ground has built up and is now dry across the mouth of the gulch. The sluicing operations of the Carissa Gulch were carried on around the clock, (usually by Chinese labor who earned a lucrative dividend of around $40 per day per man, with the price of gold at $18.75 per ounce) while the property could be operated, in the spring months of the year.

We will now cross South Pass Avenue, and we come to a monument erected to mark the location of the Esther Morris home and office. This monument was erected by the State of Wyoming while Nels Smith was governor, to replace another rather unsubstantial one erected by Capt. H.G. Nickerson. The new granite marker is embedded in a concrete base, on which a bronze plate designates it as state property and provides penalty for destruction. The plate is secured to the foundation by means of expansion bolts set in cement in holes drilled in this base. A Rock Springs man, Joe Wepner, was with the State Historical Commission and came to attach the plate. He used a

Monument dedication. Gov. Nels Smith.

Monument dedication. Mrs. Lenore Harnsberger Stone.

HOME & OFFICE SITE OF
ESTHER HOBART MORRIS
FIRST WOMAN JUSTICE
OF THE PEACE
IN THE WORLD
FEB. 14, 1870

AUTHOR WITH W. H. BRIGHT
OF THE FIRST
EQUAL SUFFRAGE LAW
DEC. 10, 1869

Esther Morris monument.

star drill borrowed from the Rock Springs Telephone Exchange to drill the holes, and after drilling about half an hour he came to the blacksmith shop where I was working and asked what was wrong with his method of operation, because after half an hour of work he had hardly made a mark on the stone. I was operating the forge and did not want to quit to help him just then, so it was agreed that I would do the job for him sometime in the next few days. He took his hammer back but left the drill, as I did not have one small enough for the job. He gave me a jar containing cement to put in the holes to assure good bondage of the expansion bolts, and a dollar to pay postage to return the drill by parcel post to the telephone company in Rock Springs when the job was completed. The following afternoon, I did the job in about half an hour and returned the drill as agreed.

We have walked down the north side of South Pass Avenue only from the place where Price Street begins, so now we will go back up the street and consider the buildings on the south side. Price Street started from South Pass Avenue in front of the White Swan and runs south up the hill past the cemetery.

CHAPTER

V

The first building on the southeast corner of the Price Street-South Pass Avenue intersection was the Wells Fargo express office, built back over the creek with log-crib support for the back of the structure. It was a log building with the customary board front. A branch line operated on a regular schedule to convey the mail from the Overland Trail, leaving it at the Burnt Ranch on the Sweetwater and coming to South Pass City either two or three times a week.

The next building was a large building, with a lean-to on the west side, made of logs on the sides and back. A wall of logs formed the east side of the larger building, functioning as a partition between the larger building and the lean-to. A doorway was cut into the larger room on the partition wall, and the lean-to room was used as a card and game room for the saloon operated in the larger building in later years. A mushroom-shaped gong bell was rung by a jerk on a string attached to a spring-mounted hammer. This notified the bartender that the low man wished to convey his order for drinks, which were on him for the game. The larger room was built of logs at the sides and back, and had a shiplap front, although the upper part had an A shape rather than the usual square front with cornice. As one corner of the building extended back over the creek channel, a log crib filled with rocks served as the foundation of the southwest corner and center of the back of the building. The larger room was once the J.W. Illif & Co. bank, where gold dust was purchased from the miners and exchange sold in all principal cities in the United States and Europe. When the bank moved its offices from South Pass, the building was used as the Exchange Saloon. There were J.W. Illif-operated banks in other locations, and a town in Colorado bears the name of this banker. A board approximately ten inches wide and eight feet long was mounted on the roof ridge, and the letters could be distinguished yet in 1950.

The ceiling of this building was of pine boards about eight inches wide. They ran lengthwise of the building, and batten strips about three inches wide were used over the board joints. I often looked at a bullet hole in the middle of the ceiling and thought how exciting it would be if one could have witnessed the events surrounding it. It was in this building that my grandmother's brother, George McOmie, was shot and killed in a card game. George came to South Pass from Nevada, and was a great help to grandmother in those hectic days when she was left with a family to care for after grandfather passed away. George was in his twenties and had been in South Pass only a few years. Evidently he had had some unpleasant altercation in Nevada, and it was my father's firm conviction that a stranger, unbeknownst to George, had been hired by Nevada enemies to commit the crime. He enticed George into a card game, contrived accusations and dispute, and drawing his gun, he shot George. The criminal was arrested and incarcerated in the county jail. Sentiment was great against him, and a mob formed to lynch him. Jim Smith, who later became grandmother's second husband, was jailer and marshal in South Pass. Hearing of the plot, grandmother in her devout Christian and characteristically kind and sensible manner, interceded. She said that her loss was already great enough without having this man's blood on her hands, and she knew that in living with his own conscience and Divine judgment, the man would receive his just punishment. Accordingly, arrangements were made and the man, Al Tomkins, left the locality, to appear no more in the region. When young, my older brother was fond of playing cards, and I recollect often how grandmother would say that we might well spend our time in a better manner than playing cards. I now understand her feelings in this respect. It was in this bar that cowboys were drinking when the Antone Stubo incident occurred.

A barbershop with a railing and slightly elevated platform was set up in the northwest corner of the room. On the east side of this building was a platform made of logs hewn on two sides, which ran the length of the building, spaced properly so that empty beer barrels were rolled on them, and which were then taken back to the breweries for refilling. Grandmother acquired this building and operated the saloon. Father served a short time as bartender. Then Orsin Grimmet leased the saloon and operated it for a while before going to Lander.

I had always thought it took a long time for wood to petrify, but under proper conditions, the process is not so lengthy. My father found a board under this building that extended out into the stream. The board had a two-inch mud and dirt covering when he found it, and it was well petrified.

The building occupying the adjoining location was originally about the same size as the saloon, but it was set back farther from the street and at about a thirty-degree angle, in a northeast and southwest direction to the bank building. One of the logs embedded in the earth was still visible when I left South Pass, but the building was razed to make room for the construction of the Grecian Bend Saloon next to the Sherlock Hotel. The saloon was afterward replaced with an addition to the hotel. The original hotel was completely torn down and rebuilt as nearly as possible to the original specifications by the Wyoming Recreation Commission. The work was so well done that only those who spent many years in the original building could detect a slight variation. The addition on the west side, replacing the Grecian Bend Saloon, was done about 1889. (The carpenter was a man named Sheldon, who later moved to Riverton. He was the father of a man who became district judge of the district in which South Pass was located.) Part of

Two Peter Sherlocks by the front step of Sherlock Hotel.

Back steps at the Sherlock Hotel. Landlock salmon trout caught at Christina Lake in 1927.

Jim Bridger visits with Janet Smith on old stomping grounds.

Jim Bridger and Lola Homscher in old car at hotel.

the hotel addition was used as office for the hotel. Behind it was the dining room, and the kitchen was at the rear. A utility shed was added to the back of this building later. The building had shiplap siding, a compo-board lining, and a ceiling of painted beaded metal. The ceilings were high in all the rooms, dining, kitchen and office, perhaps ten feet. Meals were served family style for fifty cents. The hotel had a traditional high, square front, with a cornice at the top. A door to the adjoining building, about two feet away, was connected by a short hallway from the northeast corner of the office, and another hallway and door were located in the dining room. The space over these hallways and between the buildings were closed in at the ends, and a drain ran from the buildings to the rear of the building on a metal roof, which was slanted slightly toward the back. The old hotel building was built by Ervin, who also owned the building east of it. The latter was a two-story frame house made from lumber sawed by the local sawmills and was a two-story structure. Before the new part of the hotel was built, the lower story was utilized as a dining room in the front on the west side, with the kitchen at the back. The stairway and partition divided the east and west sides of the building, and on the east side in front was a room that was used as a post office and store, later as a parlor, and still later as a bedroom. Behind this were two other bedrooms.

The upper story had nine bedrooms for customers, the one at the head of the stairway on the west side being a larger, deluxe room.

The hotel was operated for a very short time, perhaps two or three months, by Mrs. Ervin, after which it was idle until grandmother leased it in 1873. Left with a family of small children to support, grandmother was obliged to look for a means of making a living. The circuit judge, Jesse Knight, was not pleased with the dubious sanitation of the facilities operated by Mrs. Kime. Phillip Harsch, a family friend, prevailed upon grandmother to lease the unoccupied building and operate the hotel. Restaurant and hotel equipment was at a very low mark in South Pass stores, and consequently Mr. Harsch took grandmother to Atlantic, where they chanced to have a better supply and where she made the necessary purchases.

This business continued to operate for more than fifty years until decline in business made a profitable operation impossible and the hotel was closed. The store with post office across the street continued until it was sold in 1948.

The postmaster in South Pass City absconded with the postal funds and Jessie Knight acted as postmaster until John Morrison was appointed; he did so against his desires, and only to keep mail service available to the town. After serving perhaps four or five months, he persuaded grandmother to accept the position. He resigned and she was appointed postmistress, and the room mentioned before was used to accommodate the office. There was a letter drop in the front door where letters could be mailed after office hours. As it was necessary to have someone always available to care for the postal business, a limited supply of groceries was stocked to supplement the duties and income, and this was the beginning of a mercantile business that later became the Smith-Sherlock Company. The Colter & Houghton store, the first store to operate in South Pass City, was acquired; the hotel and mercantile businesses were then moved to different locations. With the acquisition of the store, the post office was moved across the street to the southwest corner of the store building, and later moved to the new addition when it was built. I believe this postmastership was in the immediate family longer than any post office in the state of Wyoming, a period of over seventy-five years. It was served first by Janet Sherlock; then by her son, James Ernest Smith (who was later the postmaster in Riverton, Wyoming); by another son, John Sherlock; and later by a grandson, Donald Sherlock; and myself as the last of the family to serve until November 1948.

With careful, frugal management, grandmother was able to feed her family during these trying years. She told me that sometimes the family evening meal consisted only of bread and milk, but she never had to send her children to bed hungry. Her brother, George McOmie, gave about the only help she ever received and his untimely death cut his assistance short. Marriage to Jim Smith did not offer much relief, in fact was a source of worry and anxiety. Dan Carmody told me Smith was a very overbearing and disagreeable man to be around when he was drinking. Given his duties as marshal or constable, his drinking caused much concern, while he contributed little to the maintenance of the family. Once when the Rock Springs band was in South Pass City on a goodwill and trade promotion program, they were headquartered at the hotel, and when they went to pay for their lodging, Smith told them that they were the first band he had heard since he was mustered out of the service at the conclusion of the Spanish-American war, and that the services were on the house. Smith made two trips to England in efforts to promote stock sales in a mining corporation; this met with little success. As the two children by this second marriage grew up, there was a great deal of favoritism. My father and uncle never talked very much about their stepfather except to say that he was mean to them, and this state-

Rock Springs band at hotel on good will tour and some South Pass residents.

ment was corroborated by what I was told by Dan Carmody and Lon Poston, who knew the family in the early days. Smith had my uncle Peter, the oldest boy, driving a string team of eight teams (16 head) of horses at the age of fourteen, hauling freight from Bryan, Wyoming (which was the depot before the U.P.R.R. lines reached Rock Springs or Green River). This was no small job for a fourteen-year-old boy—not only the work, but because of the danger from Indians and the lawless element in the country. For this reason, the Sherlock boys soon found employment in the community and left the home fires to be on their own.

I have digressed from our journey down the streets of South Pass City, as I believe many of my readers may find something of interest in my story, but now I will revert to our original purpose.

The next building was the two-room log structure with the high, square board front which was built and operated as a general store by Irvin. The partition between the rooms was of logs, and both rooms were lined with kalsomined muslin, as was the ceiling. On the east side of this building was a lean-to. There may formerly have been some other type of building here, as this was only a shiplap board shed.

At the next location was another store, although I do not know what type. It was gone before I can remember. However I had a small garden on this spot, and once while I raked the spaded soil in preparation for planting, I noticed what I thought was a copper penny. Upon removing the soil clinging to it, I discovered it was a minted $2.50 gold coin. It probably fell through a crack in the floor in this early day store.

The original buildings lining the street up to the Washington Street intersection were gone, and anything there now is of recent construction. Close to the southeast intersection corner was a fair-sized building set somewhat back from South Pass Avenue and at an angle in a northeast-southwest direction. It was operated as a pool hall and game room. The building is gone, but some of the logs were incorporated in a later building erected farther east and closer to the avenue front-

Irvin House (store).

age. The logs were halved and the corners notched, so the flat side of the logs formed the inside walls of the building. The corner notching on these logs was of the slanting beveled type, thus making the logs exert pressure toward the inside, with the notch locking in both directions. This structure was only about half the size of the building from which it was made, the pool hall being about thirty feet long. This smaller building was razed to be reconstructed across the avenue by John Woodring when he owned it, but it was only partially reconstructed. To get an idea of the values of business locations in South Pass City, an offer of twelve thousand dollars was refused for this business, and at that time, this amount of money represented a sizeable sum.

The law offices of Baskin and DeWolf occupied the next lot, but this building is gone and the present structure is composed in the front portion of logs from the Antone Stubo residence. The back part was made of logs that were in the Wygal (later William Carr) house which stood farther up the street, and were moved here by my brother Don, to make a garage for his car.

The next building is what I believe is a fairly accurate reconstruction of a theatre, or playhouse, on this location. This reconstruction was made by the Wyoming State Recreation Commission, from research and investigation by Tom Schaffer, who was caretaker at the time. He studied notes given to Grace Raymond Hebard, an educator associated with the Wyoming State University at Laramie, by my grandmother, and made on-the-spot observations. The old theatre provided the camp with recreation and amusement in the early days.

There were several wells along this side of the street, from which the residents secured their water supply for household use.

The buildings are all gone along this side of the street to the east, but in the 1920s a building was moved from Price Street to about where the South Pass Avenue and Jefferson Street intersection was. This building, once a blacksmith shop, was not very well constructed and is falling down. It is now the property of the State Recreation Commission.

About four or five lots below this building is where the Episcopal Church stood. The building was purchased and dismantled, then rebuilt with a few more logs to give additional height to the Janet Smith (afterward called the Smith-Sherlock) store.

The next building within my memory was a small, low log structure used as a barn. This stood west of the Esther Hobart Morris home that we mentioned earlier. The barn was used by Dumphrey when he stayed in town overnight.

We will now go into more detailed information concerning the person who lived in the hallowed spot east of this barn, the home of Mrs. Morris.

As I understand the story, Mrs. Esther Slack was left a widow while residing in the State of New York and afterward moved to Peoria, Illinois, and later to Wyoming, where she remarried. Because of the sex discrimination of the time, she

Peg House (right) — logs from former pool hall and Smith House ruins (east of Bilcox house). Bilcox house left with well house in front.

encountered considerable difficulty in settling her dead husband's estate, which vividly illustrated this gross discrimination, A certain amount of experience gained in operating a millinery store in New York added to Mrs. Slack's business acumen, and as she was a very able and intelligent woman, the discrimination was very distasteful to her. Therefore we can easily understand how she quickly perceived an opportunity to do something to rectify this discrimination. South Pass City was within the boundaries of Carter County, Dakota Territory. A movement began to organize another territory to give more convenient and localized government to the region and its expanding population. In the process, election districts were organized to elect the necessary candidates to the territorial legislature. Captain H.G. Nickerson and William Bright nominated as opposing candidates to the territorial legislature. At this time, Esther Hobart Morris gave a tea party, and to be sure that the successful candidate would be in attendance, she invited both. It was not a large party, perhaps about fifteen or twenty, with females very much in predominance. I do not know who the invited guests were. My grandmother was invited but had to decline because of a sick child. Mrs. Chittin and Mrs. Baldwin were among the guests. At the party, Esther Hobart Morris requested a pledge from the candidates that whichever one was elected would introduce and work for legislation granting women the right to vote and thus have a voice in the government under which they lived. How could a shrewd politician refrain from such a pledge, realizing the feminine influence in the home upon the head of the household? So that there would be no undue advantage to the opponent, both candidates gave their pledge, and thus the impact on the nation may have been as great as that of the famous Boston Tea Party. Knight was the victorious candidate, and when the legislature convened, Mrs. Morris made it a point to remind him of his pledge and to assist him in drafting a suitable bill. The talk of the town centered about this tea party.

When the bill was introduced, it caused considerable laughter and an active lobby headed by a South Pass attorney,

Strunk, worked against it, but the bill passed and received the Governor's signature, thus making Wyoming the first state in the union to render the ballot available to women. When the bill was introduced, a justice of the peace who was also the first schoolteacher in South Pass, J.W. Stillman, stated that if this foolhardy bill became law, he would resign from his judicial capacity. He tendered his resignation with the enactment of the legislation. This created a vacancy in the office, and Esther Hobart Morris was appointed to fill it.

The just and impartial conduct of Esther Morris and her ability as justice of the peace is evident from the fact that of the almost eighty cases that came before her, two or three were appealed to higher courts, and in those cases her judgments were upheld. As to her impartial dealing with all offenders, it is said that when her husband imbibed to excess on one occasion, he was brought before her court on charges of drunkenness and disorderly conduct and was sentenced to incarceration in the county jail. I cannot vouch for the authenticity of this story, but I have no personal doubt that it is true.

Esther Hobart Morris had her office in her home, which was a small, unpretentious two-room cabin, probably with the usual dirt-covered roof. In these surroundings, there was probably little to distract her attention, and true and unbiased justice was probably more equitably rendered than in many of our modern courtrooms today.

We should now go back up to Price Street and consider some of the buildings there. A little behind the buildings on Price Street, on the south side of Willow Creek and on the west side of the street, was a beer garden. One of its amusements was a swing constructed to accommodate four people, two on each side of the two facing seats. These seats were attached to an iron rod passed through holes in the arms and fastened to the upper framework, thus forming a pivot that left the seats suspended a short distance above the ground and giving the swinging action. Two men and their fair ladies could rock back and forth while sipping their beer, procured from one of the two breweries operating in the town. The

Capt. Nickerson, one of candidates at the tea party, conferring with Janet Smith.

proprietor of this enterprise is said not to have shown any preference in brands, as both brews made from the excellent local water were very palatable and of high quality.

Another form of amusement was a croquet court. The balls were about the size of a billiard ball. The arched loops were about a foot high, and the mallets about four inches long and one and a half inches in diameter, with a dowellike handle three-quarters of an inch in diameter and thirty inches long. Provisions were made for pitching horseshoes and other recreations of the time.

CHAPTER

VI

The first building on the west side of Price Street that was standing within my memory was a log building with a frame construction front, squared to the top of the ridgelog. It had a double door, with large windows on either side, and the lumber was vertical, with battened joints. The sides were of logs as was the back with the mortised-and-tenion construction. This building boasted the first shingle roof in the town. It was perhaps forty feet long and about half that in width, and had a single door in the north corner in back. It was one of the earlier establishments in the town and housed the Ticknor General Merchandise Store; it was later acquired by the Smith-Sherlock Company in a somewhat dilapidated condition. It was used for many years for the storage of baled hay, and an ice bin was constructed in the northeast part of the building large enough to store about twenty tons of ice, packed in sawdust, to provide ice for summer use. This ice was secured from a pond constructed on Willow Creek. In later years, it was easier to get the ice from the beaver dams around town. Some of this ice was sold, but much of it was used in a well-insulated room, where an ice compartment was constructed overhead. This served as refrigeration for quarters of beef. There was such a walk-in type refrigerator in the northwest corner of the Ervin Store. The baled hay was secured from hay meadows on

Sweetwater and hauled to town with four-horse teams a distance of about eight miles. Hay was one of the items of trade for the store.

The northeast corner of this building was close to the line of the townsite as surveyed by the Federal Gold Mining Company, at the southwest corner of the tract deeded to Smith-Sherlock Company and now owned by the State of Wyoming.

There were two if not three other buildings north of this building and south of Willow Creek, but they were gone before I can remember, perhaps before I was born. I do not know what businesses occupied them, or if they were residences, but the city meat market was on Price Street and may have been one of them, as their advertisement lists for sale and purchase beef, game and vegetables at the Price Street address.

At least one more building, possibly two, occupied the lots south of the Ticknor Store before my time, but the next building now standing was at the intersection of Price Street and Grant Avenue. It was of log construction. The square frame front had a single door in the center and windows of six panes of ten-by-twelve-inch glass in a sash, and a double sash in each window on either side of the door. A lean-to room was apparently added later at the back of this building. A millinery business was conducted here for a short time, if not by Esther Morris, at least under her management. She had a similar business before coming to South Pass, so had experience in this line. The building housed a saloon, then was remodeled and occupied as a home for a family named Warner, and later yet, owned by a bachelor, Ed Walsh, for a couple of years.

The east side of the street was probably occupied, but the only building I remember was a barn and adjoining carriage shed. One year when the cordwood supply of the Carissa Mine was exhausted in the spring and snow blocked the roads to the mountains, this building and other unused houses in the town were purchased and utilized for wood to furnish fuel for the boilers for the Carissa Mine. This situation occurred again several years later, when another barn built also of logs and situated on the south side of Grant (Smith) Avenue in line with Price Street, was likewise purchased for fuel.

There was a road up the draw east of this barn and another a short distance west which went up over the steep point on the west side of the draw. The latter was used in the winter months. The south part of the main road that was used for the early traffic through the town angled southwest from the Price-Grant Street intersection in a direct southwest course to the crest of the hill on the south side of Willow Creek Valley. In later years, a dugway was constructed around the point west of the winter road, and this is now the most traveled road out of town.

A log house was located close to the foot of the hill west of the winter road and dugway intersection. It was one of the early buildings in the town and several cases of the measles were isolated there in an epidemic in later years, after which it was known as the Pest House. The bachelor, Ed Walsh, lived for several years in this building around 1910.

The only building standing on Grant (Smith) Avenue west from the millinery shop is the county jail. When the prisoners incarcerated in the rock building on C Street removed some of the stones from the south wall and escaped, they were apprehended and returned to town and lodged in another building, but this demonstrated the need for a building constructed in a more substantial manner, so a log building was erected. This building was made with tenioned and mortised joints, the back logs being the length of one log and the sides, the length of two logs. The two joined logs were mortised and tenioned to a hewn and squared upright log. The door was a substantial double-board door made from one-inch lumber. There was a good-sized window on either side of the door. The building faced south on the street. The inside was lined with two-by-fours nailed together with square wrought-iron nails. The two-by-fours edgewise and vertical made a four-inch lining inside the log building, as well as the floor and partition between the rooms in the front and back part of the building and the parti-

Warrner House.

The Pest House.

tions between the cells. A layer of squared logs was laid over the top of the back half of the cell block and day room, as a ceiling. Four cells, also made of two-by-fours nailed edgewise, formed the partitions and were beveled for the doors, which were of same construction, with heavy iron hinges and hasps. The cells were about three by six feet in size. An opening about eight by ten inches in the upper part of the door served as the windows. These windows, one in each cell, had three-quarter-inch iron rods spaced horizontally about two and a half inches apart, which were incorporated in the construction of the door. In front of the cells was the day room. There, three-quarter-inch iron rods formed the grill for the two windows, about two and a half feet square, that were situated on either side of the door. The door between this cell block and the front room of the jail was also a four-inch beveled door. An opening about a foot square at the right of the door was covered by a three-eighths by one and a half inch strap-iron grill that could be opened to pass food in to the prisoners. The hasp-type fasteners on the doors were fashioned from the three-eighths by one and a half inch strap iron and an eye bolt to accommodate the customary heavy padlock of the day. The cell block and day room of this building have very good insulating qualities and are usually cool in the summer heat and less vulnerable to the erratic temperature changes in the winter. They might well be designated the "cooler," as a jail is sometimes referred to.

Provisions were made for a small stove in the day room and a small opening in the ceiling about fourteen inches square for the stovepipe. The heat in the room at the front had to be depended on to warm the back portion of the building, and as there was no glass in the openings, heat and ventilation were no great problem.

The front room of the building was used as a schoolhouse at one time after the county seat was moved to Green River, but only for a short time. A part of my father's education, which consisted of the first three grades in school, was received in this building. The bared openings were boarded up, and on the top board covering the opening on the east side of the door, was the word "study." Above the door in the front of the building was a sheeting of two-by-sixes nailed vertically. On these boards was the alphabet neatly written in Spencerian style in letters about six inches high. Several other buildings in the town were used as schoolhouses during the early years, and apparently none of them were used very long or continuously until a building designed and built for this special purpose was constructed, perhaps in the 1890s.

The night cells had numbers 1 to 4 painted on the doors, from west to east, and it was in cell No. 3 that a Chinaman committed *hari-kiri* by disemboweling himself with a case knife on his supper tray. It was his custom to continually keep up a ki-yi wail from the time of his incarceration until his suicide. While my uncle and Dave Tweed were passing the jail, uncle noticed that the wail had stopped and notified the jailor. Investigation revealed the suicide. He was accused of assaulting a white girl with intention to rape, but the suicide relieved the taxpayers of the expense of a trial. Another incident where this expense was saved was when a certain individual, never definitely identified, passed the jail about dusk, and dismounting in front of the building, removed a sawed-off shotgun from the scabbard hung to his saddle horn, entered the front room of the building, and fired both barrels through the bars of the day room, instantly killing the lone occupant, Polly Bartlett, and disappeared down the street. On another occasion, when the jail was occupied by only one inmate, a fire which caused extensive damage on South Pass Avenue broke out. The man managed to get out, presumably through the small stovepipe hole in the ceiling, and helped to fight the fire. After the flames were extinguished, he returned to jail and patiently waited for his hearing on his petty charge, to pay his debt to society. This man later served in the armed forces in the Spanish-American war, and A.C. McDowell, who lived in the South Pass area, knew him. He told my uncle that this man (whose name my uncle could not remember) was in a skirmish on San Juan Hill and was the only man killed in the skirmish.

Jail exterior.

Jail interior.

Another inmate of the jail was a man who had committed a petty crime. By some means he devised a way to open the door in the jail between the day room and the outer office room—just how, my uncle could not figure out. My uncle would bring sticks, string, and paper and pass it through the bars, and the man would make kites for him. When Peter would come the next day, the kite would be leaning against the outside wall, ready for the breeze. On one occasion, he asked Peter if he would like to come in and visit. Peter was told to go out and return in about five minutes. Upon his return, the door was opened and Peter went in. Tom Tweed, who lived up the street a short distance, evidently got a glimpse of Peter going into the building because when he got to the building, he looked for Peter, who quickly hid out of sight. As soon as Tom was gone, Peter had to leave and never got to make another visit.

All of the buildings on Grant or Smith Street west of the jail are gone, but the Boss Tweed house on the south side of Grant Avenue a short distance below where C Street ends on Grant Avenue can be located yet by the remains of a dugout in the hillside. It was in this part of town where the Sherlocks lived at the time my father was born, and so did Finn Burnett.

A window pane was accidentally broken at Finn's place and had not been replaced, so a pillow was stuffed in the hole until repairs could be made. Finn's wife awakened in the night, and was greatly alarmed at what she saw. Arousing Finn from a very sound sleep, she pointed to the window and whispered, "Indians." Sure enough, there in the slight breeze was the tip of a feather waving in the moonlight. About half awake, Finn asserted, "I'll fix the son of a bitch," and crawling from his bed, he reached under the bed and grasped the handle of the old trusty thundermug, a common fixture in every house of that day, and with a vigorous swing, took the entire lower sash of the window out. Inspection revealed that the feather was one that had worked out of the pillow, and the presence of an Indian was a false alarm.

Down Grant Street east of Price was the Black Horse Livery and Sales Stable, where saddle horses or carriages and teams could be rented or bought, and horses herded day and night or fed in the barn. This was located on the north side of the street, and Willow Creek provided water for the stock.

There were houses on the south side of the street, but they were all gone before my time. Excavations in the hillside would show their location if it had not been obliterated by bulldozers.

The large excavation which was filled with cans dumped in it for years from the hotel, and which has been covered by dozers, was the location of the brewery operated by a German named Adam Henry. Water for the brewery operation was obtained from a well at the front of the building on the east side. The top of the rock cribbing was visible in 1948 but is obliterated now. It was in the fall of the year, probably in November, when Henry went to draw a bucket of water from this well. It was icy around the collar of the well and an accidental slip on the ice evidently caused him to fall, head first, into the well, where he was found the next morning by some of the townspeople.

A short way below the brewery was a charcoal pit enterprise. A pit was dug, a fire built in the bottom, the pit then filled with wood, and this covered with dirt. The wood would slowly char, thus furnishing charcoal for the local blacksmith and wheelwright shops. At that time, the wood supply was as close as the hillside, which was timbered. A winter's wood for the operation of the hotel was secured from the stumps on this hillside one winter by my grandmother. Some of the timber was cut when there was considerable snow on the hillside, so the stumps were high. This wood harvest yielded about thirty cords of wood.

There were some houses east of the charcoal pit, but I have no knowledge of them. The remains of a rock fireplace were visible in 1948.

A blacksmith shop was located on the north bank of Willow Creek between Grant Street and South Pass Avenue, behind the Black Horse Livery and Sales Stables. In going from

Carissa Hill a short distance from where Washington Street crossed the crest of Flag Pole Hill, a street branched off around the hillside to Custer Avenue. The buildings were all gone before I arrived, but some foundations indicate their locations. They were probably residences. Custer Avenue probably extended the full length of the city, paralleling South Pass Avenue.

On the hillside above the first schoolhouse where Old Man Stillman taught school are the remains of fireplaces and some of the rock walls of buildings that were on Custer Avenue between C Street and Washington Street.

On the northeast corner of the Washington Street-Custer Avenue intersection stood a building constructed of logs for the sides and back, with a square frame frontage. The logs were tenioned and mortised on the front of the building and dovetail-notched at the back. A crib of logs flattened on two sides formed the framework for rock cribs about three feet square and about the same height, at the end and center of the base log on the south (downhill) side of the building. The front was of upright boards, with the batten boards on the joints. There was a cellar in the back of the building and also a lumber and slab dugout under the floor, about six feet square, located between the center and back log crib, with entry from the outside of the building. It was evidently used to store non-freezable goods. The construction of this building would indicate that it may have been used as some kind of a business location. It was one of the buildings in the town that was also used as a schoolhouse for a short time, and in later years was utilized as a hay storage house for baled hay from the Sweetwater Ranch by the Smith-Sherlock Company. It was known as the Brown House, and later, the Hay House. A street angled northeast off Custer Avenue east of this house and went around the hill, where it merged with Jefferson Street and then joined the street that came down Carissa Gulch. A log barn was located on the east side of this intersection. It was a two-story affair, with the hay loft or upper story at the street level of Jefferson Street and the lower story excavated at the hill end.

Rock House on Custer Avenue.

The entrance was at the ground level on the street from Carissa Gulch. The house must have been twenty feet or more in depth. These buildings belonged to a man named George Volmer. He was a large man often referred to as Big George. He was of German descent and a relative of L.L. Giessler, who operated a general merchandise store in Atlantic City. George often freighted for Giessler, bringing merchandise for the store from the U.P. Railroad.

Big George was engaged in the business of hauling freight to the mines from the railroad. His equipment was not the best. His tugs were often fashioned from inch and a quarter Manilla rope. It usually took him about three or four days longer than the other freighters to make a trip to the railroad. On one trip, while crossing the Sweetwater at Burnt Ranch, the water was rather high and his horses got tangled up. Only by quick action and cutting the tugs was George able to rescue them. With some additional knots in the tugs, George finally completed the trip.

Children's ideas of fun often take troublesome turns and involve danger to them and others. My older brother was given a single-shot .22 caliber rifle by my aunt, with instructions to keep it until he was old enough to learn how to properly use a gun. Who was to determine when he was old enough was not specified, but our decision was that he had reached that age. By putting the gun barrel in the leg of his overalls and keeping the stock under his coat, he could remove the gun from its place behind a trunk in the bedroom. Slipping a box of ammunition out of the stock in the store was not difficult, and our marksmanship was improving at irregular intervals, but there was one trifling defect in our operations. We neglected the cleaning of the gun barrel, and one day we fired the gun and the bullet did not emerge from the barrel. In the ammunition stock was a .22 caliber shell manufactured like a shotgun shell. It was loaded with small shot, about the size of a common pinhead. We inserted one of these in the gun hoping it would expel the impacted bullet, but it also lodged behind the former shot. To get more power to blow it out, another bullet fired.

This failed to dislodge the obstruction, so the gun was taken again to its customary place behind the trunk in the bedroom, and target practice was a thing of the past.

We then decided to satisfy our curiosity in seeing what would happen if bullets were caused to explode by fire. When they exploded, the lead, being heavier, stayed in the fire and the empty shell would fly into the air. Being light, they did not hurt much, even if they hit you. The shot shells, however, were a different proposition, as the shot would go in the air. On one such occasion one of these shells exploded when we were too close, and Delbert McOmie got one of the shot lodged in the lobe of his ear. In the excitement it was not noticed, but that night his mother discovered it and removed it with a needle, but could not find out how it got there. This led to suspicion on the part of our parents, and the next time we went over the hill to the George Volmer barn and built our fire, parental watchfulness disclosed the nature of our doings, so my father was notified and appeared on the scene. Our fire was kindled on an old manure pile, and a fire in a manure pile can often smolder for days before erupting into a full-fledged fire, so father was engaged in carrying water some considerable distance to completely extinguish the fire. After this strenuous exertion, our correctional punishment was not overly severe, and far less than we had earned for our misdoings.

This clue led to the instinctive reasoning of father, and he examined the Stevens single-shot .22 rifle and found that it was plugged from about six inches from the chamber to within six inches of the tip of the barrel. It took about a month for the vinegar with which the space in the end of the barrel was filled to work its way through the lead, but the task was finally completed, and although I don't think the rifle was as accurate or as hard shooting as before, it did work in a fairly satisfactory manner.

The only building now standing on Custer Avenue is the schoolhouse. It faces east and sideways to the Avenue. This building was moved from its location up on South Pass Avenue across from the Masonic Hall to this location. A few logs were added to the building by the carpenter, Ed Walsh in about 1908 or 1909 to give more height and replace the rotten logs.

All of the buildings on Jefferson Street are gone, but it was on this street that the girl lived who was the object of the affections of McGovern and Flannigan in the incident related formerly in our story. It was also on this street somewhere that one of the South Pass City newspapers had its office. There were once two newspapers issued in the city, one issued weekly, I believe it was the *South Pass News*, and the other, the *Sweetwater Mines*, issued on Wednesdays and Saturdays.

Jefferson Street extended in a northwesterly direction from the "Big George" barn to merge with C Street where it made a bend about halfway up Carissa Hill. About seventy-five yards from this junction was a shaft that had a log cribbing around it about four feet high, and back of this was a log dug-out with a dirt roof, in which the owner of the mine, Reilly, lived, and so it was known as Reilly's Cabin.

Another set of buildings that may properly be included as part of the town is the Carissa Mine buildings. The original log building was a shaft house, and when Bolivar Roberts owned this mine, the ore was hauled with teams and wagons to a ten-stamp mill below South Pass. This mill was operated by water power, the wheel being about thirty-four feet in diameter and probably thirty inches wide. It was an overshot wheel, and water was carried in a ditch from Willow Creek along a side hill through a flume that led from this ditch across the road to the top of the wheel. There was sufficient flow in the stream to operate the ten stamps, which I believe were fifteen-hundred-pound stamps, about two months of the year, and the one battery of five stamps for an additional thirty days. The ore was transported from the mine and stockpiled, mostly during the winter months, and milled in the spring of the year. My father hauled ore two different winters for Roberts. While engaged in hauling the ore, he lived in the house later occupied by the mail contractor, Albert Bayers, at the west end of South Pass Avenue. To qualify for the job, a person had to have a tight

School House on Custer Avenue, 1909.

School 1916-17.

wagonbox and, a canvas of a fourteen- or sixteen-ounce weight to cover the bottom. Some of the dust would sift through the canvas, so after unloading the ore, the wagonbox was carefully swept, and these sweepings were then panned and as high as $80 in gold was sometimes recovered, with gold price then at $18.75 per ounce. In sinking the original shaft on the Carissa vein to a depth of one hundred feet, the ore yielded an average of over two hundred dollars per ton. The records of the U.S. Mint credit the production of the Carissa Mine as close to a million dollars. Bolivar Roberts took out over a million dollars, and a more likely figure of the production would be between two and three million dollars. There remains low grade ore of close to a half million dollars blocked out in the workings that will someday be worked when the value of gold allows a profit margin in extraction. I have a letter from Roberts, written to my uncle, in which he states that if he had a million dollars, he would invest it all in the Carissa Hill. When he sold the mine, he went to Ogden, Utah, and went into the drug store business, but it was not as profitable for him as his mining ventures. It was at this time that he wrote this letter to my uncle. This mill was destroyed by fire, and it is my belief that it was then that Roberts sold the mine. A Negro was employed as watchman at the mill, and when the building caught fire, in his excitement and fear, he ran barefooted and dressed in his underwear only, to South Pass, loudly shouting, "The mill is on fire." The building burned to the ground, but the large wheel and the timbers supporting its shaft and bearings were well watersoaked and remained standing until the 1930s. After this incident, a vertical shaft was sunk to the one-hundred-foot level on the Carissa vein, and a shaft house and steam-powered mill were erected at this location south and west of the original shaft.

There was also a residence for the superintendent, and another two-room log building for a caretaker. After the death of the principal owner of the Carissa Mine, who was also the president of the corporation, the heirs sold the mine and under the management of a man named Thorne, the Dexter Mining

Bolivar Roberts water power wheel on Willow Creek below South Pass.
The mill was burned.

Bolivar Roberts mill at Carissa Mine constructed after Willow Creek mill burned.

South Pass City, showing Carissa Mine as it was when Dexter Mill was moved from Atlantic City to Carissa Mine.

Company mill in Atlantic City was purchased and this mill and building were erected in place of the original structure. This installation provided for cyanidation of the tailings from the mill to provide a more complete recovery of the values from the ore. The shaft house and hoist house was again moved to a location east of the discovery shaft, and the ore transported by a conveyor belt to the mill ore bins. A superintendent's residence, a bunkhouse, and a boardinghouse were also built, as all the boarding facilities in South Pass were closed at the time. These are the buildings that now stand at the mine.

This constitutes a resume of the buildings that existed or that 1 have knowledge of, around 1960, in the town of South Pass. But sites of former buildings are visible along Willow Creek, above and below town, and some of them are connected with historical events that hold a certain interest for the people in the locality.

CHAPTER

VII

On the north side of Willow Creek above town, just about across from the mill building mentioned in the early part of our story, is a tunnel cribbed with rock and timber, back to the solid rock ledge, beyond which timbering was unnecessary. This was known by the townspeople as Uncle John's Tunnel. (The man who dug it was named John.) A footpath followed along the creek in front of this tunnel that was used a good deal by the miners who traveled between the Wyoming Copper Mining Company mine and South Pass. As there were no leads or veins of ore uncovered in the face of the tunnel, it was not driven very far into the solid rock and was abandoned. A carpenter named Smith, referred to by the residents as Smithy, and employed by the Wyoming Copper Mining Company was overtaken by the urge of nature, and entered the tunnel to obtain privacy to answer the call. While thus engaged, Smithy observed two shining disks in the darkness of the tunnel that seemed to be coming toward him. The law of self preservation superseded any call of nature, and Smithy barely reached the mouth of the tunnel ahead of a badly frightened lynx cat that took off in the brush while Smithy proceeded down the trail at a swift pace, slowly gaining his composure and arranging his raiment. Upon reaching town, Smithy related the incident to his listeners in his loud and boisterous voice, declaring that "A man is taking his life in his hands in this country." As a carpenter, Smithy's work could be identified by the fact that his joints were made to stay, the nails driven in until the ends of the two-by-fours were usually well split and cracked.

A short way up the creek, on the south side of Willow Creek above the mill site, was a neat, two-room log cabin with a dirt roof. The corners of the logs were dovetailed and neatly trimmed. There was another poorly constructed small house; rocks built up for a forge inside indicated that it was utilized as a shop. This was probably erected by a person who had a brick kiln. The site is very close to the railroad grade across Willow Creek where the road crosses on its way to the U.S. Steel iron ore mine and upgrading plant.

Above this on the north side of Willow Creek was an arrastre which must have been powered by an undershot waterwheel, as the ditch carrying the water came out of Willow Creek a short distance above, not far enough to give sufficient fall for an overshot wheel.

Farther upstream was the location of another arrastre, and this one had an overshot wheel.

Here gulches come into Willow Creek from both sides, and the bottom is wider. On the hill south of the stream is the location of the mine that belonged to the Wyoming Copper Mining Company under the management of a man named McFarlane. This mine was the best copper prospect I know of in the district, and had some very promising ore for a depth of about one hundred feet, below which it diminished in value until at the bottom of the workings, the rock was barren. This shaft was on a considerable incline and the upper shaft could be traversed on foot for some distance. It was the deepest shaft in the country, five hundred feet deep. There was a shaft house and a hoist house at the mine, and at the foot of the hill was a boardinghouse. The boardinghouse was purchased by A.C. Crofts and moved to a ranch that Crofts purchased from W.E. Kenyon, about two miles northwest, further up on the main fork of Willow Creek. The shaft house disappeared some time earlier.

About half a mile above this copper mine, Willow Creek

Wyoming Cooper Mining Company boiler ready for transportation.

Tom Brady's freight team.

forks into the main fork and the south fork. A small temporary cabin was built just below the forks, by a few men who were engaged in cutting wood for the Carissa Mine. The wood was used to fire the boilers, providing the steam power to operate the mining machinery. It would probably be impossible to locate the ruins of this cabin now, but among the occupants was a young greenhorn unaccustomed to the ways of the western mining camps. Any entertainment or amusement had to be provided by the ingenuity and imagination of the gang, and as the evenings were long, it was the custom of the fellows to relate tales, often real but some with a flavoring of imagination added to provide proper atmosphere and enjoyment.

Bear tracks were seen around the cabin, and this led to the telling of bear stories in the camp, and some uneasiness and apprehension was observed in the young man. These stories were continued again on the following nights for a few nights. Meanwhile a bear hide had been obtained and secreted in the camp, so when the atmosphere was ripe, one of the men placed the bearskin on his back, after all had retired for the night. Then, on all fours, he went to the greenhorn's bed and managed to contact his hand with the fur. Awakening from a sound sleep and in silent fright, the greenhorn recalled how some of the tales told that remaining motionless and playing possum had been the means of avoiding a bear attack. Not a sound was heard. The bear went out of the cabin without molesting anyone or anything, but in the morning, the cabin door was open and, sure enough, there in the snow were the tracks of the departing bear leading into the wood.

The young man left the woodcutter's camp that day.

The Little Hermit heads east of the present Highway 28, and the Big Hermit heads in the Dunbar Meadows west of this highway. These streams run together east of the Carissa Mine. The stream is then known as the Hermit, from this junction to Willow Creek, below South Pass City. Over the hill, east of Hermit Forks, is the head of a gulch that runs parallel to the Hermit and is known as Vinegar Gulch. It runs into Willow Creek, not more than a hundred yards below the mouth of the

Hermit. A cabin constructed of rocks was located at this intersection of Vinegar Gulch and Willow Creek, between Willow Creek and a ditch that carried water to operate the early Carissa mill further down the stream. This house was gone and not noticeable from the road within my time, but the foundation and a portion of the lower walls can be found. This cabin was built and occupied by a man named Frances Zeriner. He had a partner in several of his mining claims, Sam Fairfield. Zeriner was a man of quiet, sober and sour disposition, wholly unable to appreciate the humor of a joke, and from this characteristic, he was known in the community as Vinegar. Hence the name Vinegar Gulch was used to designate this particular gulch. A disagreement arose between Fairfield and Zeriner over one of the claims, and Fairfield went up to his house in town and returned with his rifle. Zeriner was walking toward his cabin away from the rocky outcropping on the road, a short distance from the back of his cabin, when Fairfield returned and shot him in the back, killing him instantly.

An arrastre was located downstream from the mouth of Vinegar Gulch but above the old Carissa Mill that was destroyed by fire, and another one was located below the mill not far above where the road crossed the stream and went over the hill on the south side of Willow Creek above the rocky canyon. Between the mill and this lower arrastre was a two-room log cabin, probably built in the 1880s. One year when activity in the South Pass Country was at a low ebb, in the early 1900s or before, my uncle grubstaked some miners, about seven: Charlie Bluitt, A.E. Hinkley and some other Englishmen who came from the same locality in Wales, and who were known as cousin Jacks, or cousin Welshmen. They were to work on the Carrie Shields mine on top of the hill at the head of the draw that comes into Willow Creek where the cabin was located. The miners lived in this cabin while working on the claim that winter. They built a horse-drawn whim to hoist the ore from the shaft. It was constructed by erecting a timber vertically with bearings at the bottom (floor) beam and a bearing at the top, or rafter beam, of the hoist house. Two sets of spokes, or crossarms, were attached to the vertical shaft, and a wooden rim was fastened to them. Two-by-sixes were nailed to these rims, making a wooden drum about thirty inches long and about eight feet in diameter. This was made at the upper part of the shaft.

A beam was attached to the bottom of the vertical timber, extending out to a circular pathway below the outside of the drum. A singletree was attached to the end of this beam, and a workhorse was led in this circle to revolve the drum. A manila rope one and a half inches in diameter was fastened to the drum, of sufficient length to pass over a pulley wheel over the mouth of the shaft and to the bottom of the shaft, with some extra in case of sinking the shaft to a lower depth. The horse was kept and fed in a shelter provided at the bottom of the hill, close to the cabin, at night. Prior to this, the ore had been hoisted by the old windlass method, operated by manpower.

This is the only mine I know of in the district where this novel horsepower hoist was used. In the operations by the Welshman, they placed a shot in the footwall of a drift to widen the tunnel in their operations, and in so doing, hit a streamer off the vein which carried considerable values. The result was that the winter's operations produced sufficient ore to pay for the grubstake, a reasonable profit, a fair wage, and employment for the miners.

I do not know who the original locator of the mine might have been, but one of the owners in earlier times was N.L. Turner. He was a promoter as well as a miner, and was considered a windbag and blowhard by the residents. I had a day book, which was left with some of the other books in the store. His name was on the outside cover, and the book contained some notes and figures, but most of the pages were blank. One page contained a notation that he had sold a third interest in a mining claim in Butte, Montana, called the Little Darling, for $300. When Ray Tower was in charge of operations at the Carissa Mine in the 1940s, he told me this was one of the oldest and richest claims in the Anaconda claims there. Ray was a metallurgist in that section employed by the federal

Ruins of Carrie Shields' whim.

government, and so was acquainted with the region where he worked. A family named Shields were living in South Pass then. There was a son, Tony, and two girls, Carrie and Mary. Turner was a suitor for Carrie's hand, and so called the mine the Carrie Shields, and he may have well been the original locator.

Later, this claim was leased or sold to a well-known character in the district, about whom many tales are related: Samuel O'Mera, of Irish descent. O'Mera employed Sam Ryder and my uncle Peter when he worked the claim. My uncle and Sam Ryder worked in the shaft and O'Mera hoisted the rock from the hole with the windlass. This was the most strenuous part of the work, but he was one given to hard work and was practically untiring. On one occasion, Ryder said to Peter, "It seems to me it must be about quitting time." Peter agreed, so they decided to climb the ladder out of the shaft. When they reached the surface, the stars were all out. O'Mera was asked why he had not told them when the day was over. He said "I thought you wanted to work, so I was willing to work with you." O'Mera told Peter that after taking the lease and option to purchase on this claim, he noticed something he had not noticed when he made the deal, and it was not until sometime after that that he observed the gold in the vein resembled shaved gold coin that appeared to have been loaded into a shotgun shell, where the shot had been removed, and this shot into the vein. This is the only time I ever heard of this method being used to salt a claim. Sam's conclusion as to the gold coin shavings was undoubtedly correct. It was some time after this that Peter and his half-sister, Anna Tibbals, acquired the Carrie Shields.

Farther down Willow Creek, where the country is less rugged and the stream bottom widens, was another enterprise that was operated in the early days, and while it was a financial success, it operated for a short time only. Stephen Bartlett operated a saloon and dance hall in Cincinnati, Ohio. Hearing of the great opportunities in the Oregon Country, to which many were then migrating, Bartlett decided to go to what he believed to be greener pastures. At this time, his family consisted of a daughter, Polly, rather good-looking and in the early stages of womanhood; a son not yet in his teens; and Polly's first cousin, a niece of Bartlett's, Hattie, who served as housekeeper for the family and nighttime partner for Bartlett, whose wife had either left him or was dead. Polly was perfectly willing to let cousin Hattie do all the household drudgery, which was done without complaint.

Arriving in Colorado, the Bartlett family spent some time there before resuming their journey along the trail to Oregon. Before leaving Denver, they purchased some arsenic which they used to sprinkle around outside of the tent walls to kill the ants, mice, and rodents. Eventually they arrived at the place where the Emigrant Trail forked at Sweetwater and came north of Sweetwater for a number of miles before joining the main trail, at the Burnt Ranch crossing. The Bartletts took this branch. When they got to where this branch crossed Willow

Creek, they decided to camp for a few days to rest their stock, and pitched their tent a short distance upstream. In those early days of sparse settlement (1867), travelers were sociable and it was common custom to visit without the formalities of acquaintance or introduction. Lewis Nichols, who had been prospecting and mining gold with some success and was returning east, stopped to visit at the Bartlett camp. Preparation of the meal was in progress and the aroma of the frying buffalo steak caused Lewis to remark that he would give ten dollars for a good steak meal. Polly told him that she doubted if he had ten dollars to pay for a meal. Lewis assured her that he had been fortunate in his mining activities, and to assure her, he produced a roll of greenbacks. The perfect plan flashed through Polly's mind, and she assured Lewis he would have his steak meal for ten dollars and she would cook it for him. This steak was sprinkled well with the powdered arsenic and the meal was served, but before finishing it, Lewis became violently ill and soon died in convulsions.

The money would be easy to handle but disposition of the body was more difficult. Bartlett dug a shallow grave in the stock corral and buried the body. He was then ready to break camp and move on along the trail, but Polly informed him that this was not the plan, that they would locate on the spot, as this was more profitable than any business that they had ever been in. The location was ideal. The Overland Trail followed up the Sweetwater to where it crossed the Continental Divide and then proceeded to Pacific Springs and on to the Sandy's and Green River on the western slope of the divide. With the heavy travel along the trail, the stock would find little forage, the emigrants would cross to the north side of the Sweetwater at St. Mary's crossing and follow up Silver Creek, then past Diamond Springs, across Strawberry, Rock and Willow creeks, and join the trail on the south side by crossing at the Burnt Ranch on Sweetwater. This trail provided additional feed when the original trail was grazed off, and there was much travel on it. Bartlett built a house to provide more adequate facilities for their enterprise. They called it the Bartlett Inn. He also constructed a barn with a hayloft, and corrals for his horses and cattle, from logs and poles cut in nearby groves of pine.

The fact that a resident of the community, Lewis Nichols, had mysteriously disappeared did not arouse undue suspicion, as it was some time before it was learned that he did not arrive at his intended destination. Also, it was not uncommon for a person to come to an untimely death in those days.

Timothy Flaherty, a drummer (as a salesman who often acted as a collection agent for his company was then commonly known) represented a wholesale establishment in Omaha. He had been calling on his customers but failed to return with his collections and orders, and an investigation revealed no clues as to his disappearance. A twenty-nine-year-old cattle buyer had a brother living in South Pass City. He would come into the region to buy cattle and often carried considerable sums of money to make his purchases. He stopped at the Bartlett Inn, and Polly craftily and cunningly ascertained the nature of his business, as well as the fact that he probably carried considerable cash to conduct his business. This was Polly's usual course of action, to determine if the traveler would be a profitable victim, after which she would display all her feminine charm to lure her intended victim. She took him out to see the Bartlett cattle, then invited him to accompany her to the hayloft in the barn to enjoy a good time. In a country where there was such a scarcity of the female sex, her proposition was very enticing. In the loft, he heard someone enter the barn, and soon Bartlett's head appeared through the opening in the floor to the loft. Bartlett had climbed the ladder and held a double-bit axe, which he leaned against the wall in the loft. He also had a pint of whiskey, which he placed on the loft floor, telling Polly it was for her use in entertaining her friend. He then departed. Polly urged the cattle buyer to have a drink, but was assured that he was a total abstainer and would not have a drink, in spite of Polly's taunts and ridicule. Polly was very much frustrated when her plans failed to work, and she informed him that she was not used to dealing with anything but real he-men and that she would have nothing to do with Sunday-school boys who did not drink or swear. The cattle buyer went down into the barn, saddled his horse, and resumed his journey. Arriving in South Pass City, he detailed his experience at the Bartlett Inn to his brother. Another resident of South Pass City, Edmund Ford, was expecting his brother and received information that his brother had arrived at the Bartlett Inn, but as there was no further information, Edmund surmised that he had been the victim of Indian savagery or had been ambushed by one of the numerous bands of road agents.

Bernard "Barney" Fortune, a blacksmith from Missouri, arrived in South Pass City with the gold rush and had been successful in his mining ventures. His son, twenty-three-year-old Theodore, who was receiving his schooling at Albright College in Reading, Pennsylvania, was scheduled to arrive in South Pass City about August 14, 1868, for a short visit with his father before returning to his studies at the college. Upon his failure to arrive after some time, and when his departure was confirmed by a letter from Barney's sister in Bellvue, Nebraska, the Pinkerton Detective Agency was employed to trace Theodore on his journey. The agency sent three investigators, well trained in the work in this frontier country, and Theodore's trail was easily followed to the Bartlett Inn, but here it disappeared completely. Barney Fortune, Sheriff Lombardi and his deputies went to the Bartlett Inn to question the members of the family. Polly related that she remembered the young fellow very well and liked him a great deal. With profuse tears streaming down her face and cheeks, she had warned him of dangers from Indians and thieves in night travel and had pleaded for him to wait until morning to continue his journey to South Pass City. A thorough search of the Inn and surrounding country by the sheriff's party in the next few days failed to reveal any clues as to the possible whereabouts or evidence of foul play to Theodore Fortune.

Carl Armentrout, another traveler on his way to South Pass City, where he had relatives, also was known to have mysteriously disappeared about this time. Reflecting on the similarity of these circumstances, Sam Ford became suspicious and voiced his suspicions to Sheriff Lombardi. They decided to make another search of the country and Bartlett Inn. It was made without any results, but evidently Bartlett's better judgment dictated that he should move on and not remain with the finger of suspicion pointing at him. The next day, a trail boss, Billy Gordon, reported Bartlett's departure, who in his haste, had abandoned his cattle. This prompted another more thorough search of the house and barn. When the searchers were about to give up again, fresh digging was discovered where the cattle had eaten all the hay covering it. Investigation revealed that this was Bartlett's method of concealing the evidence. He would bury the corpse in a shallow grave in the corral, then feed hay to the cattle over it. Twenty-two bodies were found, and that of Edmond Ford was identified by a Masonic ring with his name etched on it. Fortune's body was identified by a gold belt buckle that had been presented to him by his father. The buckle had the appearance of being made of brass, so its true value was not realized by Bartlett or removed from the body. It was a present from Barney, made from gold from Barney's mine. Greatly saddened, although he had gained considerable wealth, Barney declared that he wished he had remained in his blacksmith shop back in Missouri. Barney posted a ten-thousand-dollar reward for Bartlett, and the territorial legislature also approved and posted a three-thousand-dollar reward. Several men searched for Bartlett to claim the reward. Sam Ford reasoned that Bartlett would leave the main trail but would continue to head for Oregon, where he had originally planned to go. Locating what he believed to be their trail, he followed it, and seven days after their departure from Willow Creek, Ford found the Bartletts in the Hoback River Valley. Arriving at the night campsite, Ford carefully made his way to it. Ford ordered Bartlett to put up his hands. Bartlett went for his gun leaning against a nearby tree, but Ford's shot killed him instantly before he could reach it. With the situation in hand, Bartlett's body was lashed to the saddle and the party proceeded back to South Pass City, where Polly was turned over to Sheriff Lombardi, and Hattie and the boy released to continue their journey. It is probable that Bartlett occupies one of the unmarked graves in the cemetery on top of the hill south of town. Ford appropriated the il'-gotten money the Bartletts had, and claimed the rewards. Polly was confined in the county jail to await trial, and on October 7, 1868, a person greatly resembling Otto Kalkhorst, a mine boss and foreman employed by Barney Fortune, of German descent, rode down Smith Street at dusk with a sawed-off ten-gauge, double-barreled shotgun slung by a loop of rope on the saddle-horn. Reaching the jail, he dismounted, entered the front room, and quickly discharged both barrels of the shotgun through the bars in the day room of the jail, striking Polly and killing her. Her body is also likely buried in the cemetery beside her father's grave. This prompt action saved the taxpayers the expense of a trial and rope, as well as rendering true justice.

Ford afterward married Sally, a daughter of Sheriff Lombardi, and homesteaded on Sandy near the present town of Farson. Here he built up quite a profitable cow ranch operation of around three thousand head and built several houses, but later, Cheyenne Indians raided and murdered the family there, burning the buildings and killing or stealing the livestock.

Indian depredations were frequent in the South Pass country, but in its short existence, Bartlett Inn was never raided. It was theorized that this was due to the fact that when a victim fell to the ruthless hands of the proprietor, his horse and personal belongings were given to the Indians, thus gaining their favor and also removing evidence of the deplorable cruelty and ruthlessness of the Bartletts. The evidence would point instead to the Indians.

It was on the hills between Bartlett Inn on Willow Creek and Rock Creek, in the Lightning Springs area, where my uncle Peter had his closest brush with the Indians. He was perhaps fifteen. The freight teams were often ranged on these hills when not making a trip to the railroad for freight. Peter was riding to look after them when he was spotted by a small number of Indians in war paint. He started for home but was losing ground when he saw a couple of other riders who chanced to be in the country, and he rode toward them. The Indians then gave up the chase, as they did not care for an encounter with such small odds. Their group had made a couple of killings in the country a few days before.

My uncle related a story of the trails, about an incident on the Oregon Trail near the Burnt Ranch. A band of Indians were traveling along the ridges quite a way from the trail but parallel to it. This was not a party of warriors, but just a group with women and children along who were going to a new camp. They were traveling along single file. A young man in his twenties was traveling in the band of emigrants. Thinking it was too distant to do any harm, he fired a shot at the Indians for no apparent reason than to see what they would do. The shot hit a squaw and killed her. The infuriated Indians rode in front of the emigrant train on the trail and demanded the person that fired the shot. It was the chief's squaw who had been killed. They threatened an attack on the train if the guilty person was not apprehended. The young man realized the folly of his actions but it was too late. His surrender would mean almost certain death, but resistance by the train would probably mean several deaths. He knew his friends would support him and it was a difficult choice; in fact, he felt that he had no choice, so he surrendered to them. He was placed on his horse between guards, with his hands bound behind him, and the party proceeded to the camp ground for the night. The emigrants set up camp a short distance away. At dusk, the Indians built a large campfire. The man was bound to a stake set in the ground. The braves in their paint would dance their war dance around the stake and come in with their knives and skillfully remove a small patch of skin from his body until after several hours of this torture, there was little skin left. He was released and helped on his horse and allowed to ride back to his friends in their camp. He requested a smoke and a blanket, saying he was cold, and in a short while he died from the ordeal of being skinned alive.

Indian depredations were numerous in the country, and one incident that has some connection with South Pass City and its residents may be of interest. It concerns a trip made by Uncle Ben Hurst and Dave Hays. They were bringing a load of groceries and supplies to South Pass for William Tweed. A yoke of oxen were hitched to the wagon. About ten miles below the three crossings on Sweetwater, a night attack was made by the Indians, and Hays, who had his bed on the ground, was shot. Hurst was sleeping in the wagon and the Indians did not see him. Hurst got out and stood the Indians off, and after several assaults, they withdrew. Hurst made a breastworks of rock and left Hays with gun and ammunition and taking the oxen, departed for South Pass City to get help. As soon as Hurst left, the Indians made another assault, killed Hays, and helped themselves to what they wanted from the wagonload of groceries. Hurst was an English sportsman and an excellent shot and managed to keep the Indians at a safe distance as he drove the oxen before him to South Pass. Upon arrival at South Pass, William Tweed, who was a nephew of Uncle Ben Hurst, William Rose and Mike Welch departed to go to see about Hays and the abandoned wagonload of goods and also the wagon. Hurst was to follow with a three-yoke team of oxen to haul the wagon home. When they got to the wagon, they found little left of the supplies, as a Mormon train had passed through, buried the body of Hays, and helped themselves to most of what was left of the supplies. After four days' wait, Uncle Ben Hurst arrived in company with Major Noyes Baldwin, a South Pass merchant who was on his way to what was then the terminus of the Union Pacific Railroad construction, a place called Benton. With Baldwin were two drivers, Van Camp and Leach, and two passengers whose names I do not know. Baldwin had two yoke of oxen to haul the freight. The Indians attacked them at Ice Springs on Sweetwater, and they had to retreat back to South Pass, where they arrived safely as Baldwin had stood up in the wagon and kept up a steady stream of fire. Hurst received a wound in the heel and Leach was wounded in the back. After several days' wait at the wagon, the teams arrived and Tweed, Rose and Welch started back for South Pass. They were again attacked at Three

Crossings on Sweetwater. Welch's horse was shot from under him but he managed to escape into the brush on foot. Rose had a very fine, spirited horse and he felt confident he could outrun the Indians, but they overtook him and shot him in the back of the head, killing him instantly. Tweed was riding a mule, and in the excitement, the mule bucked Tweed off. Tweed shot one of the Indians with his shotgun, cutting the body almost in two. Running through a break in the line of the surrounding ring, across a swampy marsh that was too soft for the indians' horses to follow, Tweed reached the Sweetwater. He fortunately found a wash and undermined bank, and crawling into the water under the bank, eluded the Indians, who after many hours of searching, abandoned the hunt. Tweed made it back to South Pass in a couple of days with only a slight wound in the back.

One of the first corporations, if not the very first in the Territory of Wyoming was a company incorporated to build a toll road between South Pass City and Atlantic City, by Manafee and Fry. Its offices were in Atlantic City. Another road that reached more than the drawing-board stage was a toll road from the Atlantic City-South Pass City road at a point between Little and Big Hermits, to go west up Slate Creek. Washington Mallory Hinnman had a sawmill located on Slate Creek, and a townsite planned just above where the present Louis Lake Loop road crosses Slate Creek. I believe some of the organizers associated with him in the Slate Creek Road were the same as the Atlantic City-South Pass City road organizers. I do not think they were included in the townsite project. There were only a few houses built in this venture.

Another toll road to the Lewiston and Miners Delight (Hamilton) district was planned, but I do not think it materialized. Hamilton was the name given to the town when it was first formed a short distance from the Miners Delight discovery, but the town was known as Hamilton for only a short time, and it became more generally called Miners Delight by the people in the locality. Eventually the town automatically assumed the latter name.

A few words might be in order here relative to the South Pass band, which was organized before the turn of the century. Most of the men in the town were members, and latent ability was brought to life in some whom you would least expect to perform. I never thought Little Joe Basco had even a trace of musical ability, but I was assured by my father that he was a definite asset to the band. At one time, among the membership were five men who had some experience in leading a band. With this reserve to call upon, the band was never without a leader. Those judged competent to fill this office included Charlie Bates, Alvin Phillips, High Shears, and Charlie Bluitt. Charlie Bluitt often played the accordion for the dances in South Pass. High Shears was very proficient on the slide trombone.

CHAPTER

VIII

I have endeavored to give you a picture of the town and of some of the stories connected therewith, as well as some of the actual historical events of which I have firsthand knowledge. Before closing, however, I would like to recount for you, a story or two as written by my uncle Peter, one being about an incident in the Palmetto Gulch Placer.

The early pioneers of the South Pass country had to face many hardships and annoying inconveniences, but their greatest worry was an ever-present dread of surprise attack by the many bands of hostile Indians, who at frequent intervals invaded the region. This mental strain was occasionally relieved by some humorous incident that afforded the pioneers a good laugh and a little relaxation. One of these incidents occured when, in the summer of 1868, John Johnson and six or seven other prospectors organized themselves into a co-partnership to work some placer ground that they had located in Palmetto Gulch, about two miles east of South Pass City. Their first project was to construct a ditch about three miles long to bring water for sluicing purposes to the placer ground. They then set up a camp near a spring, a short distance from the ground where their mining operations were to be carried on. After the completion of a few other preliminaries, they were ready to begin washing gravel.

It was the practice of such small co-partnerships operating placer ground to sluice for a week or so and then to clean up and weigh the gold recovered and distribute the proceeds equally among the partners. No deductions were made for time lost due to sickness or to any other unavoidable cause. This was the practice followed by Johnson and his associates.

The work moved along quite satisfactorily until one morning one of the partners complained of being sick. He was told by the other partners to remain in bed and rest up, and that he would probably be feeling better by the next morning. He accepted their recommendations and acted on their advice, not only for that day, but for several days thereafter. He did not appear to be suffering any serious pain and he would get out of bed and eat a hearty meal equal to that of any of the other men, after they had prepared it for him. After each meal, he would again roll up in his blankets and remain there until called for the next meal. The other partners stood this for a time, but they began to suspect that working with a pick and shovel in the mud and water and a strong aversion to such vigorous exercise were the chief causes of the sick man's indisposition. As they discussed the matter one day, while walking back to work after their noonday meal Johnson said, "Leave him to me. I will find out how sick he is." Nothing more was said at the time, and they were all soon back at work, but all the men kept their rifles within easy reach while they worked, and after working for a short while, Johnson picked up his rifle and started to crawl stealthily toward the camp. Concealed by the growth of sage brush that covered the ground, he approached to within seventy-five yards of the tent where the sick man lay. Taking careful aim, he aimed over where he calculated the sick man's head would be and fired a shot over the prostrate form. With the crack of the rifle, the sick man leaped from his bed, and in great fright, abandoned all reason. Barefooted and clad only in his underwear, he bounded away over the rocks and through the brush down the gulch toward Willow Creek, a mile or more away. Johnson fired another shot as the terrified fugitive disappeared down the gulch. He returned quietly back to work, remarking, as he laid aside his rifle, that the fellow made a good race for a sick man.

The panic-stricken man raced madly down the gulch, paying no heed to the rocks, snags and brush obstructing his way until he reached Willow Creek, where, turning up that stream, he continued his flight for another quarter of a mile, to where the Carissa stamp mill was in operation. There he presented a sorry spectacle, with his undergarments torn to tatters, his feet cut and bruised, and his legs scratched and covered with blood. After regaining his breath, he told the men employed at the mill that his camp in Palmetto Gulch had been attacked by Indians and that all his partners had been killed. He alone had escaped by flight. After listening to his report, the men at the mill took their rifles and hurried up the long hill north of the mill. They crossed the ridge and proceeded down into Palmetto Gulch where the placer ground was located. There they found the placer miners working as usual, and when they told the placer miners of the report which had led them to come up from the mill to investigate, they were informed that their partner had not been well for several days, that he had been remaining in camp, where he must have had a bad dream, as they had not seen any Indians.

The sick man now had some real injuries to nurse, but his injuries, while painful, were not serious, so that within a week or so he was able to return to his work, and from that time on, throughout the season, he did no more shirking. This incident was the source of considerable ridicule and jibes at the young man. Even his girl friend lost interest in him, and he left the district in the fall of the year.

To add spice to community life, a character, John Ahlberg, worked at the Carissa mine; he was a large angular man of Norwegian descent. A fellow countryman who came to the district soon after arriving in this country, had a great deal of communications difficulties, and John endeavored to come to his assistance. He found the fellow to be a very poor student, as he had not mastered his native tongue in a very creditable manner, or had forgotten it. After painstaking and time-consuming efforts, John could not seem to make much headway, and finally his patience was exhausted. "I feel sorry for you, you poor damn fool," exclaimed John, "You left your country and forgot the language and came to a new one and did not learn its language."

Ahlberg was very good-natured and not easily angered, but like most people of such disposition, when angered, he could be a force to be reckoned with. The men employed at the mine carried lunches for their mid-shift lunch break. These lunch buckets bore little resemblance to the present day lunch boxes. They were usually round, a little larger than the present-day No. 10 gallon can in which foods are packed, and were made of tin or graniteware. The drink, usually coffee, was put in the bottom of the pail, then another container which fitted inside the bucket occupied about half the depth of the bucket contained sandwiches, sometimes pickles and cheese. Another shallow pan then went in the container, to carry pie. This was then covered with a lid on the top of this lid, a strip of metal, about an inch and a half high formed a circular upright collar soldered to the lid. A low, metal cup, complete with handle fit snugly over the collar. If this pail, which one carried with a bail, was placed in a moderately warm place, the coffee often remained warm until lunchtime.

A fellow worker had some limburger cheese in his lunch bucket, and he shaved a thin slice from it and cautiously placed it in Ahlberg's hat, under the sweatband. When Ahlberg put the hat on, the heat greatly enhanced the odor, and whenever anyone came close, they would sniff and move further away, avoiding Ahlberg as if he had some kind of plague. This continued for several days and all the time, Ahlberg was vainly trying to determine the source of the foul odor. At last he managed to ferret out the offensive item and vowed that he would make sure that the s—of a b—would never be able to play a dirty trick like that on him or any other person again. Considering the nature of the man, everybody knew he would not stop short of murder, as it was not an idle threat, so silence reigned supreme and Ahlberg never did find out who the guilty culprit was.

I would not consider my story complete without including

another of Uncle Peter's accounts, as I have found these very interesting and believe they may prove to be the same to you.

The early settlement of the town of South Pass City was never marred by the spirit of unrestrained lawlessness that prevailed in many communities, during the early pioneer settlement of the western country. Shortly after the town was started, peace officers of undoubted courage and grim determination to preserve law and order were selected and installed to conduct the affairs of the town. Their job was performed well, but in spite of this there would be an occasional incident in which individuals with differences took the law in their own hands and undertook to settle their controversies by the primitive method of deadly personal combat.

One such encounter occurred in the summer of 1869, in which a young man in South Pass City received a shot through the shoulder, which shattered the bone and severed an artery. South Pass City at that time had three resident physicians, but all of these happened to be out of town when the shooting occurred, and as the wounded man was bleeding profusely, it was imperative that the help of a doctor be secured without delay. A messenger on horseback was dispatched to ride with all possible speed to Atlantic City, to call a doctor from there. When the messenger raced into Atlantic City, he found that Dr. James Irwin was the only physician in the town, and Dr. Irwin positively refused to answer the call of the wounded man in the neighboring town until the payment of his fee had been guaranteed. As the messenger was unable to furnish such guarantee, he was compelled to return to South Pass City and report his failure to secure medical aid. The unskilled persons attending the wounded man did what they could for him, but they were unable to check the flow of blood. He grew gradually weaker, and expired from loss of blood within a few hours.

Not long after the tragic shooting affray in South Pass City, Dr. Irwin's twelve-year-old son started out to walk from Atlantic City to the town of Miners Delight. He took a direct trail, leading over the hills and across the gulches, the distance between the two towns, by that trail, being only about three miles, and as there had been no recent report of Indian raids anywhere in the district, the short trip was not considered dangerous, but the boy had proceeded only a mile or so on his way, when, as he was crossing a gulch in the bed of which there was a considerable growth of willows and small aspens, a band of Indians suddenly rushed from the brush and quickly surrounded and captured him. They stripped him of his clothing and then told him to run. The terrified boy, thinking that having robbed him of his wearing apparel, the Indians might possibly intend to inflict no further harm on him, obeyed their command, starting off at the highest speed he could muster toward home, but the savages followed him, shooting arrows into his body as he ran. They continued this fiendish sport until they neared the outskirts of the town of Atlantic City, where they ceased their brutal torture of their helpless victim and beat a hasty retreat. Abandoned by his savage assailants, the boy slowly and painfully made his way to the town of Atlantic City, where horrified friends quickly lifted and bore him quietly to his home, but he had been cruelly and fatally hurt. Many arrows had pierced his body, inflicting grevious wounds, and one of the arrows, which had struck him between the shoulders, in the back, had passed entirely through his body, and the spiked end of this arrow protruded from his breast. Skillful hands removed the cruel shafts from the lacerated body of the youthful victim, but little more could be done for him, and a few minutes after the last arrow had been removed, death mercifully relieved his sufferings.

In the summer of 1891 Peter met a man by the name of Mason, who had been a resident of Atlantic City in 1869, but who had left there, returning to his home in Iowa a year or so later. Mason had just returned to Wyoming for a few weeks' visit to the scenes of his early adventures in the western wilderness. Recalling some of his earlier experiences in Atlantic City. Mr. Mason said that he had been intimately acquainted with Dr. Irwin, and that shortly after the tragic death of the latter's young son, the doctor had said to him, "I shall never cease to regret my action in refusing to answer the call of the young man who was wounded in the shooting affray in South Pass City. I know that I should have answered the call, regardless of whether I ever received any payment for my services, and I cannot help feeling that the sad tragedy in which my young son was taken from me was a judgment of Divine Providence, visited upon me in punishment for my failure to perform my plain duty toward an unfortunate fellow creature."

Another story of the locality deals with the discovery of the Miners Delight mine. The Carissa and Miners Delight were the two best-defined ore leads in the mining district, and the largest producers of ore that could be profitably mined.

Practically all of the discoveries of the large gold-producing properties of the South Pass country were the result of intelligent, painstaking study of the geological formations, coupled with much hard work. But the discovery of the Miners Delight, one of the most outstanding gold producers of the entire South Pass region, was an exception to the rule. As the story goes, this discovery came about in the following manner.

In the summer of 1868, a man whose chief occupation had been gambling and hard drinking, and who was just emerging from a protracted spree, wandered out into the evening in a half-dazed condition. When the man came to his senses the following morning, he found himself lying in the bed of a gulch, with no familiar object in sight. He arose from the ground and, looking around in an effort to determine where he was, his attention was attracted by a considerable quantity of broken quartz, which lay scattered over the ground, a few feet from the spot where he had spent the night. He picked up a piece of the quartz and was surprised to find it covered with many particles of gold.

He examined other pieces of the quartz and found that many of them showed free gold. Taking some of the pieces of quartz with him, he climbed the hill along the west side of the gulch, and from the top of the hill he was able to distinguish landmarks, by which he was able to readily retrace his steps back to Atlantic City. There he looked up a number of friends of his own stripe, to whom he showed the samples of the rich ore he had found, and the group at once started out to investigate the find. When they arrived at the scene, they quickly discovered that the pieces of ore scattered over the surface had been broken from a vein of the same material, the outcroppings of which were plainly visible a few yards up the gulch. They posted notices, locating several claims on this vein, and these claims became the famous Miners Delight mining property, which for a few years eclipsed in production the output of any other property in the entire South Pass country. Work was started at once on the new discovery, and the ore proved very rich from the first. Some of the ore was hauled to the Carissa Mill on Willow Creek, about a mile down stream from South Pass City, where it yielded as high as five thousand dollars per ton. The proceeds of this ore provided the owners of the Miners Delight with funds with which to purchase and install needed mining machinery and a ten-stamp mill on their property. Then began a period of a few years of bountiful golden harvest—and of unrestrained, profligate spending that consumed all profits, regardless of their size, as fast as they were realized.

This method, or lack of method, of business procedure made no provision for setting up a reserve fund, to take care of any adverse conditions that might arise. Therefore, when the rich oxidized ores were largely exhausted, and the low-grade primary ores encountered, the owners found themselves unprepared to continue work, so their mining operations were suspended and their property soon passed into other hands.

The following story clearly illustrates the manner in which the owners of the Miners Delight carried on their business during the profitable period of their mining operations.

On a winter night, in one of the saloons in the town of Miners Delight, a big poker game was in full swing. Two of the owners of the Miners Delight property were seated at the table, taking part in the game. As the night wore on, these two mining men found that they had lost all of the money they had with them. With this discovery, they withdrew from the game and hurried off up the gulch about half a mile to the mine, where they closed down the mill, cleaned a considerable quantity of amalgam from the plates, and then proceeded to retort the amalgam. This concluded, and being in a hurry to get back to the game, they removed the cover from the retorting crucible and tossed the ball of hot bullion out onto a ten-foot snow-drift to cool. The hot ball of metal, worth several hundred dollars, at once melted a hole in the snow and quickly settled down to the bottom of the drift. "Oh, let it go," said one of the men. "We can get it next spring, when the snow melts.' They then reentered the mill, made another cleanup, retorted the amalgam, and this time exercised a little more care in cooling the ball of bullion. With this task successfully completed, they took the ball of bullion and hurried back to the saloon, where they were soon again seated at the gambling table.

George McKay, who directed the milling operations at the Miners Delight mine during the few years of phenomenal gold production of that property, estimated that the production was worth fully one and a quarter million dollars.

Frank McGovern, the man who made the discovery, and one of the original owners and operators of the Miners Delight mine, made and squandered a modest fortune. He was also engaged in two gun duels, killing one man in South Pass City and another in Atlantic City. He left Miners Delight soon after disposing of his mining interests there, and was next heard of from Deadwood, Dakota Territory, where he had gone with the gold rush in 1876.

There he acquired and operated some rich placer ground, from which he realized large returns, but living up to his reputation as a profligate spender, he dissipated his profits as fast as they were received. He returned to the South Pass Country for a visit of a couple of months in the summer of 1886, and traveled to Rock Springs that fall. There he became involved in a barroom brawl a short time later, and was beaten to death, thus ending a somewhat colorful, if not distinguished, career.

IX

While the first half of the winter of 1882-3 in Wyoming had not been marked by the usual severe December and January storms, there had been a number of light snowfalls, and the weather had for the most part been cold and disagreeable. But up to January 30, 1883, the snow that had accumulated had not reached such depth as to make it necessary for J.L. Sanderson & Co., then operating the stage line to make the usual winter change, in mode of conveyance, from spring wagons to sleighs. Sanderson & Co. furnished mail and passenger service between the town of Green River, on the U.P. Railroad and Fort Washakie, 150 miles to the north; serving en route the towns of South Pass, Atlantic City, and Lander.

On January 30 a heavy storm set in along the line of this route, and as the storm continued throughout the night and was unaccompanied by wind, the snow lay where it fell, with the result that the morning of January 31, hilltop and lowland were blanketed with snow to a depth of over twelve inches. The schedule on the Green River-Fort Washakie stage line called for the trip to be made in 36 hours one way. and this was divided into three drives of about fifty miles each: a day drive between Green River and Big Sandy; a night drive between Big Sandy and South Pass; and a day drive between South

Pass and Fort Washakie. It had been the practice of the stage company to discontinue the night drive during the winter months, thereby increasing the time of the through trip to 60 hours, but because of the absence of serious snow depths up to the last week in January, the change from summer to winter schedule had not yet gone into effect. The storm of January 30 prevented the arrival at South Pass of the stage that had left Fort Washakie that morning and was due to arrive at South Pass in the evening. Because of the failure of the Fort Washakie stage to arrive, the stage scheduled to leave South Pass for Big Sandy that evening remained over at South Pass until the following morning. The morning of January 31 was dull and gloomy. The sky was heavily overcast and snow was falling, but there was no wind and the temperature was some-what above normal for that time of year. It was therefore thought that when George Ryder, driver of the stage, left South Pass for Big Sandy that morning, he would make the drive without serious difficulty. Maggie Sherlock, the eighteen-year-old daughter of Mrs. Janet Smith of South Pass was a passenger; she planned to go to Salt Lake City, where she was to attend school. W.J. Stuart; the superintendent of the Stage Company, was also on the outgoing stage, and the stage was loaded to capacity with bundles of long willows, which Mr. Stuart intended using to stake the road as he went along from South Pass to Pacific Springs. Pacific Springs was the first station out from South Pass, about twelve miles away. The road was staked by planting a willow upright in the snow at intervals of twenty-five or thirty feet along the road. The purpose was to enable the stage driver to follow the road in severe storms or when the track had become obliterated by heavy falls of snow. This was the first winter trip of a sleigh over the road, and its progress was retarded, to some extent, by the work of staking the road and the depth of the new un-packed snow. It was therefore nearly noon when the station at Pacific Springs was reached. Here Mr. Stuart remained, intend-ing to await the incoming stage and to return with it to South Pass. A change of horses for the outgoing stage was made at

Pacific Springs, and the driver Mr. Ryder, with his young lady passenger, left for their next drive of eleven miles, to the station at Dry Sandy. This drive was made without serious incident, but travel was slow because of the constantly increasing depth of the snow which continued to fall throughout the day.

By the time the Dry Sandy station had been reached, the day was well spent, and to add to the gravity of the situation, a strong northeast wind had sprung up and the snow had begun to drift. It would have been the better part of wisdom for the driver to have remained at the Dry Sandy station until the storm had abated, but Mr. Ryder insisted on going forward, and after securing a change of horses, he set out with his passenger on the next drive of sixteen miles, to the station on Little Sandy. He had gone only a short distance when he lost the road and, after some difficulty, he returned to the Dry Sandy station. Still believing that he could make the drive after securing his bearings, Ryder again set out. Shortly after the second start, the wind increased in velocity, the snow fell faster, and the storm assumed the proportions of a blizzard. George Ryder was a young man, a Texan by birth, who had come north during the summer of 1882 and he was therefore unacquainted with the rigorous winter climate of Wyoming. Soon after making the second start from the Dry Sandy station, he again lost the road, and he became so bewildered by the blinding storm that he had no idea where he was or what course to pursue to proceed on his way, or how to return to the shelter of the station at Dry Sandy. He drove about for some hours, but made little headway. The snow, which the wind now blew at a terrific rate, had piled in huge drifts, through which the horses drawing the sleigh floundered with great difficulty.

Night had closed in and impenetrable darkness added to the blinding fury of the storm. The temperature too, had dropped rapidly and the cold had become intense, but in spite of the intense cold, the smothering snow with which the air was laden was extremely wet. This is a characteristic of the northeast blizzard, and the wet snow driven by the fierce wind, adhered tenaciously to whatever it came in contact with and at once formed into a sheet of ice. To face such a storm was humanly impossible, and to travel with it, through deep drifts of snow in inpenetrable darkness, and with the air thick with whirling, wind-driven snow, was almost equally impossible. Under these frightful conditions, the team driven by Mr. Ryder became exhausted, and when he drove into a depression filled with snow, he was unable to urge the horses forward. There the sleigh remained until the storm was over. It is probable that Mr. Ryder, like most persons who are lost, had traveled for the most part in a circle, as the place where his sleigh was found after the storm was little more than a mile from the stage station at Dry Sandy, in the head of a gulch which led almost directly to the station. Mr. Ryder had little knowledge of the country through which the stage road passed, and he was therefore unable to recognize the gulch and take advantage of it as a means of making his way to the Dry Sandy station, thereby saving his own life and that of the young lady passenger who shared his awful plight.

Throughout the night of January 31 the blizzard raged with undiminished fury. Maggie Sherlock was warmly clad and well provided with wraps. Crouching in the box of the sleigh, she protected herself as best she could from the bitterly cold wind and the whirling snow. Mr. Ryder unhitched the horses and he spent the night in walking back and forth beside the sleigh in an effort to keep up circulation and withstand the penetrating, death-dealing cold. Both fervently hoped that with the light of day the storm would abate and that they would then he able to reach shelter, or that help would come to them, but the morning of February 1 broke with no cessation in the fury of the elements, and the storm continued with undiminished intensity throughout that day and the night which followed. During the day, Mr. Ryder made several futile attempts to make his way to the Dry Sandy station, hut each time he returned to the sleigh, to report to his anxious passenger the failure of his effort. He also got Miss Sherlock on one of the horses and mounted the other horse himself. They started out, hoping to be able to reach the Dry Sandy station on horseback, but this, too, proved unsuccessful. Returning to the sleigh, they decided to remain there until the storm had passed, which they accordingly did.

With the dawn of the day on February 2, the storm showed signs of breaking; the cold was still intense, but the snow had almost ceased to fall and the wind was less furious. Therefore, Mr. Ryder, although badly frozen, again set out, in a last heroic attempt to secure help. This time he succeeded in reaching the Dry Sandy station, but he was in a terribly exhausted condition and was able to give the stocktender, John Thorn, little information as to where he had left his passenger, and the horses and sleigh. Mr. Thorn, however, gained some idea of where the sleigh had been left, and with a fresh team of horses he at once started out in quest of the missing girl.

After searching for some time, Mr. Thorn finally saw the seat of the sleigh protruding from a deep snowdrift and removing the seat and digging down in the snow beneath it, he found Maggie Sherlock wrapped in a buffalo robe, still alive but semiconscious. He extricated the sleigh from the snow as speedily as possible, and hitching the team to it, he returned with the girl to the Dry Sandy station, where Mrs. Thorn received her and tenderly cared for her for several days until she could be moved to her home in South Pass.

The stage for South Pass left the station at Big Sandy on the evening of January 30 with a Mr. Scott as driver and Mr. Clark, a rancher of the Lander Valley, as passenger. The snow, which had been falling all day and which continued to fall throughout the night, completely obliterated the track, and as darkness closed in, the driver lost the road and wandered about, making little headway, until morning. With daylight, the road was located and the stage proceeded on its way toward South Pass, arriving at the Pacific Springs station about noon on January 31. There Mr. Stuart boarded the stage to return to South Pass: there were therefore, on the stage leaving Pacific Springs for South Pass, Mr. Scott, the driver; Mr. Stuart, the superintendent of the stage company; and Mr.

Clark, the passenger. Mr. Scott had suggested that the stage lay over at Pacific Springs until the following morning, as he and Mr. Clark were weary from a sleepless night and day of travel, and signs of the impending blizzard were already manifest. Mr. Stuart insisted on proceeding to South Pass, saying that as the road had just been staked, the remainder of the trip could be made without serious difficulty.

The furious northeast blizzard was encountered shortly after the stage left Pacific Springs, and although to continue on their way the three men had to face the biting wind and blinding snow, they struggled forward for a distance of eight miles, to Fish Creek, four miles from South Pass. The storm had now reached its height and the worn-out horses could no longer be induced to face it. Night had come on and impenetrable darkness added to the horrors of the situation.

The three men held a hurried consultation. It was decided that to face the storm for a distance of four miles, to the town of South Pass, would be a physical impossibility, but they thought that they might be able to retrace their steps, traveling with the storm, and reach the shelter of the station at Pacific Springs, eight miles distant.

They unharnessed the horses, who were worn out, and turned them loose; they then set out to battle for their lives in an effort to reach Pacific Springs. For a time, two of the men remained at one of the willow stakes along the road while the third went forward until he had found the next stake. He would call to his two companions, and when they had caught up with him, he would again go forward to locate the next stake, but as the progress made in this way was very slow, and as Scott and Clark felt that they could not long endure the terrible storm, they set out, saying the case was one in which each man should strive to save himself, and leaving Stuart, who because of his heavy buffalo overcoat and heavy clothing was unable to keep pace with them. None of the three men succeeded in reaching Pacific Springs during the storm.

On February 2, after the blizzard had subsided, Joe Johnson, the stocktender at Pacific Springs, started on foot for

South Pass, and a short distance from the road, on top of the divide between Pacific Springs and the Sweetwater River, about three and a half miles from Pacific Springs, he found the frozen and lifeless body of Scott. Loyal Manning, also an employee of the stage company at Pacific Springs, left the station a short time after the departure of Mr. Johnson and made his way to the top of the divide, toward Sweetwater. He hoped that he might possibly find someone who had been caught in the storm and would be in need of assistance. When he had reached a high eminence commanding a good view of the surrounding country, he saw on a hillside, some distance off to the northwest, a dark object. He started toward this object, which he later found to be only a dark rock which had been swept bare by the wind, but while traveling toward it he discovered a line of indistinct marks in the snow. Believing that these might be the footprints of someone traveling through the snow during the storm, and that the footprints had been nearly obliterated by the drifting snow, he followed the line as closely as he could. After proceeding about a mile, he came upon Mr. Stuart, lying in the bed of a deep gulch, almost buried in the snow and in an almost unconscious condition. With great difficulty, Mr. Manning succeeded in reviving him and getting him to the Pacific Springs station, where first-aid treatment was applied to his feet, hands and face, which were terribly frozen.

Mr. Clark, like Mr. Scott, perished in the effort to reach safety. His body was found a little more than a mile from Fish Creek, where the sleigh was abandoned, but being buried in a deep drift of snow, it was not discovered until several weeks after the tragedy.

The stage scheduled to leave the station at Big Sandy for Green River on the morning of January 31, with Al Dougherty as driver, delayed starting for several hours, awaiting the arrival of the stage due from South Pass. But as the South Pass stage failed to arrive, Mr. Dougherty started for Green River in the afternoon. He had proceeded only about seven miles when the blizzard struck, and so fierce was the storm that he was unable to either go forward or to return to the Big Sandy station. To remain where he was seemed to mean almost certain death. He knew that the Big Sandy River, on which the stage station bearing that name was situated, ran two or three miles west of the point he had reached with the stage, and therefore decided to make an effort to reach the stream, hoping to follow the stream to the station. He accordingly unhitched the horses, and with a firm hold on the traces, he drove them ahead of him, traveling westward, with the storm nearly squarely in his back. In this way he reached the Big Sandy River, but the fury of the storm had so completely bewildered him that he was unable to determine which way to turn in order to travel up stream. He finally got this question straightened out in his mind, but found that in order to follow up the stream he would be compelled to face the storm, to some extent, and this he felt unable to do. He therefore decided to remain where he was and, by vigorous exercise, escape freezing until the storm had abated. The low hills along the east side of the river broke the wind to some extent, and a patch of willows growing along the banks of the stream furnished a little protection. He thought of trying to start a fire, but in that hurricane of wind and with the air a wet mass of driving snow, he knew that he would never be able to get a fire started. Therefore, fastening the ends of the traces of the harness on one of the horses together, and running his arm through the loop thus formed, he drove the horses before him through the snow, alongside the patch of willows on the bank of the stream. Forward and back he drove, and followed and stumbled after the horse throughout the night and the next day and the night following, until at last, on February 2, the storm moderated.

Al Dougherty was a young man of powerful physique, but his hands and feet were badly frozen and he was nearly exhausted by the terrible experience through which he had passed. He therefore realized that if he were to save his life, he must seek aid without delay. He started up the stream, driving the horses before him and clinging to the traces of the harness, as he had done for the preceding forty hours. But the snow was deep, and horse and man were worn out almost to the point of collapse, so that progress was slow. Many times the struggling man lost his hold on the traces and fell into the snow, but with desperate tenacity, he regained his feet each time, and again securing his hold on the traces, he once more moved slowly forward. When within two hundred yards of the Big Sandy station, he fell and it seemed to him that the end of the struggle had been reached, as he was now so utterly exhausted that he could not regain his feet. However, he made one last desperate effort, and crawling, reached the station on his hands and knees.

When George Ryder reached the station at Dry Sandy, his hands, feet and other portions of his body were found to have been terribly frozen, and although Mr. and Mrs. Thorn did everything within their power for him, it was evident from the first that he could not survive his awful experience. He died on the third day after reaching the station.

Maggie Sherlock had not been so seriously frozen, but her hands, feet and face had been quite badly frosted, and the awful ordeal through which she had passed, had completely unnerved her. However, she responded at once to the rest and care accorded her at the Dry Sandy station and it seemed that she would recover. Several days passed before her family at South Pass learned of her plight, but as soon as the roads had again been reopened to travel, her stepfather, James Smith, went out to Dry Sandy and brought her home. He returned to South Pass with her on February 11. After her return home, she continued to improve for several days, giving rise to fond hopes on the part of family and friends that she would not only be restored to complete health, but that her hands and feet would also be saved from the surgeon's knife. These hopes were destined to be cruelly crushed, as the period of recovery was followed by a sudden change for the worse on February 18, and from that time on the suffering girl grew steadily worse until, on February 21, death claimed her as its shining mark.

W.J. Stuart and Al Dougherty were both taken to Green River as soon as possible after the roads had been reopened.

Mr. Stuart received medical attention in Green River and Mr. Dougherty was sent to a hospital in Laramie. Both ultimately recovered, but Mr. Stuart lost both hands, portions of both feet, his nose and both ears. Mr. Dougherty had one foot amputated above the ankle and the other at the instep; he also lost portions of most of the fingers on both hands. Both men were therefore hopelessly crippled for the rest of their lives.

Wyoming has long been noted as a land of rigorous winters. Many have seen the blizzards that have swept over her mountains across her prairies, taking their toll of human lives and leaving widespread destruction in their wake, but never since the earliest white settlers entered this region has it been visited by a blizzard equal in intensity, duration and fury to that of 1883. No record is available of the temperature that prevailed throughout the storm, as no one in the region where the blizzard reached its greatest intensity had a spirits thermometer. It is known that the temperature was far below zero, as the mercury in the ordinary thermometers descended into the bulbs and remained frozen for two days. Since the time of this blizzard, it has been the practice of old settlers, in discussing any storm of unusual severity, to compare it with the blizzard of 1883.

As a small child, I remember seeing Al Dougherty only a couple of times—Peg Leg Dougherty, as he was sometimes called. I was somewhat impressed with the way he mounted his horse, grasping the saddle horn with his left hand, which was not so badly crippled, and with a strong swing would bound into the seat of the saddle.

Another storm from the northeast that resulted in tragedy for a stage line occurred in the early 1920s. A man named Ralph Faler held the subcontract to carry mail from South Pass to Pinedale. The schedule called for the trip to be made three times a week. By spring, most of the snow around the South Pass country had disappeared except for the drifts. There was not a great deal of mail, most of it being first-class, so Faler had discontinued the use of the horses and would come as far as he could in his car, then carry the mail on foot to the South

Pass post office. Only a few drifts in the road prevented him from driving all the way, and when he would come to a drift, he would spend some time shoveling the snow, then start on foot in time to reach South Pass in the later part of the day.

He had made a couple of trips and had shoveled the drifts as far as Pine Creek, about three miles from South Pass. On this trip, which was in the later part of April, he came to the Pine Creek drift and shoveled away about half of the drift, then started for South Pass. He had a heavy coat, which he put over the radiator of his car to help conserve some of the heat so that it would start easier when he came back in the morning. It began to snow a little in South Pass about seven o'clock, and when Faler did not show up by that time it was concluded that he must have had trouble with the car or had turned back, so no one thought the matter was of particular concern. The storm continued to increase, and by ten o'clock it had assumed the proportions of a small blizzard. A deputy sheriff from Pinedale—Sorrenson—came in on the Lander stage on his way back to Pinedale. The next day the snow continued, so he was marooned in South Pass, but on the third day the storm had just about played out. Sorrenson borrowed a horse from us and rode out on the road; he found the deserted car on the south side of the drift at Pine Creek. He returned to South Pass and reported his findings. Ralph's father was an old-time freighter in the South Pass country and in the winter, when he would be idle on the freight lines, he would graze the freight team on the hills on the south side of South Pass. Ralph would wrangle the horses, and so was well acquainted with the country. It seemed inconceivable that he would have difficulty in making his way to South Pass, as the storm did not get bad until after he should have reached town. Telephone communications with Pinedale and relatives there shed no light on his probable actions. A search party was organized and close to a hundred men came to South Pass the next day and the search began.

The population of South Pass was very small at this time, and the feeding and room accommodations were taxed to the limit. After three days of unsuccessful search, all but a brother and one or two others returned to their homes. The storm had put down about two and a half feet of snow at South Pass, and there were drifts of new snow as much as ten feet deep. Iron pipes were used to prod some of the drifts in efforts to find the body. The only clues found as to the missing man's actions were some twigs and matches in a rocky point in Slaughter House Gulch, at the base of a pine tree less than a mile from South Pass, just below the regular road perhaps one hundred and fifty yards. Apparently the matches were wet, as some did not light. Being unable to start a fire, Faler started out from the faint indications of tracks, in the direction of South Pass. But the snow had obliterated all other signs. If he had been able to keep his bearings to the north, he would have come to Willow Creek, and there he would have had some shelter from the storm and could undoubtedly have made it to South Pass, as he was a man in good health and only in his fifties.

After a week the search was abandoned until the snow should melt and reveal the whereabouts of the body. Three weeks after the storm, Joe Basco, who had a place on Sweetwater close to the Burnt Ranch, came up to South Pass on horseback, his usual mode of travel. After crossing the Sweetwater and going through a gate in the fence, his dog ran down a road along the fence and began to bark at something. Joe rode over and found Faler, lying in the track of the road, the mail sack folded under his head for a pillow, his hands folded over his chest. This was a distance of about seven miles from the rocky outcroppings in the head of Slaughterhouse Gulch. In a storm it usually appears that you are walking uphill, even when there is a considerable down slope to the grade. Faler evidently got turned around in the storm and followed down the gulch.

When the telephone line was built through South Pass by the Pinedale Telephone Company, the man in charge of the construction held quite a bit of interest for me as a child. An encounter with a bear somewhere up on the Green River had left him with a badly scarred face, mutilated ears, and some hand injuries. He was known as Bear-Face Dodge.

One of the best known and highly respected missionaries in this country was the Rev. John Roberts, who came from England and established the Episcopal Indian Mission at Fort Washakie. He was an intimate friend of the great Chief Washakie and was held in high esteem by the Shoshoni tribe. Rev. Roberts was very devout and sincere in his work, and converted many members of the tribe to Christianity, among whom was the great Chief Washakie. At the chief's request upon his demise, Rev. Roberts performed the Christian burial rites, and Washakie was buried in the graveyard not far from where Roberts established his mission and Indian girls school.

It was Rev. Roberts' lot to arrive by the incoming stage in the blizzard of 1883. He was on the incoming stage from Green River and was marooned at the Dry Sandy station, where his services proved a great help and comfort to all at the station. He held the burial service for George Ryder as his first official act, as recorded in his journal. Ryder was buried in a snowdrift, where he remained until the snow began to melt in the spring, and then the body was brought to South Pass City and buried in the cemetery, and I don't think the grave was ever marked.

Rev. Roberts also cut sagebrush for the fire at the station and helped in the care of Maggie Sherlock. The large sagebrush growing in the draws was the only source of fuel for this station. After the storm, Rev. Roberts came to South Pass with Maggie and remained with her family for a few days before continuing on his journey to the reservation.

Rev. Roberts performed the marriage ceremony for my only sister and her husband at the Roberts Mission at Fort Washakie.

The blizzard of 1883 certainly was a proper initiation into missionary duties for a young man just arriving from England. It was from the Roberts Mission that the burial ceremony was performed by Rev. Roberts for the noted Indian guide who piloted the Lewis and Clark expedition across the country, known in history as the Bird Woman, Sackajawea. She is buried in the cemetery not far from the Roberts Mission. The inhabitants of the South Pass country often displayed great ingenuity in their everyday existence. A man who followed trapping in the upper Sweetwater and Sandy's conceived the idea that a bearskin would make an ideal garment for winter wear; accordingly, he carefully skinned a bear that he had killed and tanned the hide. He cased the legs and feet, which he carefully skinned out, so there would not be any holes from the waist down. During the winter months, this man busied himself with his trap lines, but in the summer he devoted much of his time to fishing in the Little Sandy stream. The fish were taken to South Pass City, where there was a ready market; fish are not native to the upper Sweetwater and its tributaries, a fact not generally known by the present-day inhabitants. The excellent fishing in these streams today is the result of early plantings of these waters of rainbow, native, cut-throat and brook trout.

One fall, after about a six-inch snowfall, two men were hunting on the Little Sandy and they came upon a fresh bear track in the snow, which they followed up the creek and soon came upon the maker of the tracks. One of them took aim and was about to shoot, but the bear traveled only on its hind legs and not on all four feet as is natural, and this aroused his curiosity. Further observance led the men to make a more careful investigation and to discover that the bear was the trapper in his bearskin garb. Thus what might have been a tragedy, left the men with a relieved feeling of thankfulness that the "bear's" unnatural behavior had prompted the rifleman to refrain from shooting.

I have tried to cover some of the arrangement of the early town of South Pass, and the more outstanding incidents concerning the houses and their inhabitants, as well as a few of the stories about the locality that I have found interesting. I trust they may also hold some interest for you.